COLLEGE SPORTS ENCYCLOPEDIAS

THE COLLEGE FOOTBALL ENCYCLOPEDIA

BY CHARLIE BEATTIE

Encyclopedias

An Imprint of Abdo Reference

abdobooks.com

TABLE OF CONTENTS

SUN DEVILS
SUN DEVILS
62
58
4

THE HISTORY OF COLLEGE FOOTBALL

The first college football game was played on November 6, 1869, in New Brunswick, New Jersey. Two schools from the state squared off. Rutgers beat the College of New Jersey, which is now known as Princeton, 6–4.

The game looked much different than it does today. Teams had as many as 25 players on the field, and those players competed without helmets. Running with the ball was against the rules. So was passing it forward. Players scored points by kicking the ball into a goal. The game looked more like soccer or rugby than what modern fans know as football.

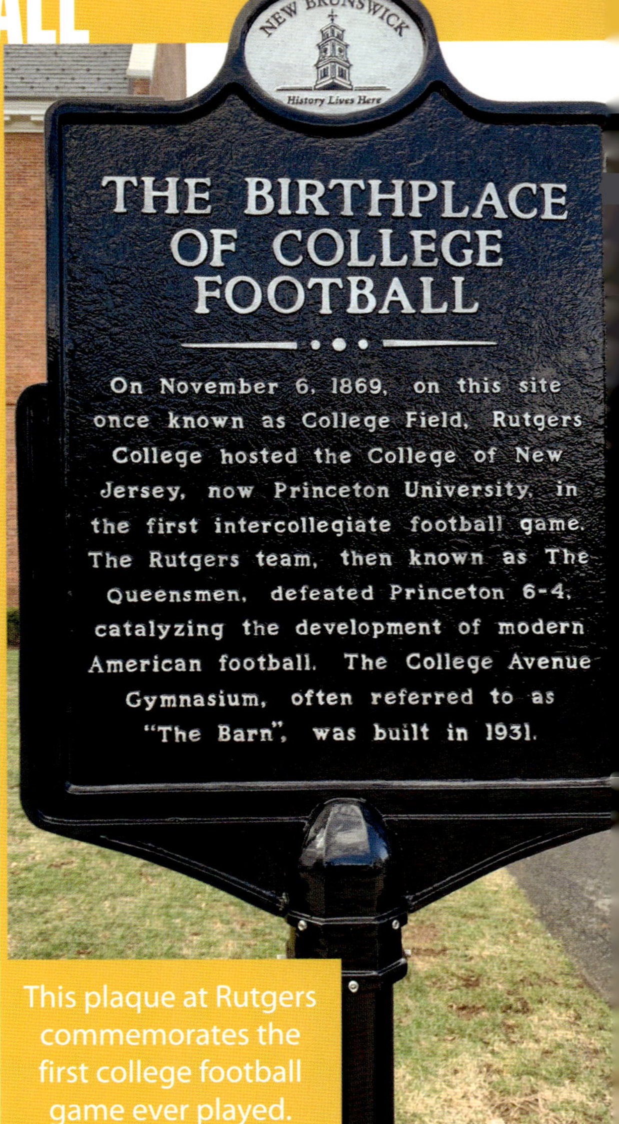

This plaque at Rutgers commemorates the first college football game ever played.

For the rest of the 1800s, the game grew on the East Coast. Most of the powerful schools were Ivy League institutions such as Harvard, Princeton, and Yale. And it was Yale's coach,

Walter Camp, who wrote the first standard rules for football in 1876. Camp's rules established the 11-man team, the system of four plays to make a first down, and six points for a touchdown. Though the game's rules have evolved over time, Camp is considered the father of modern football.

SURGE IN POPULARITY

Camp's version of the game spread around the country. Many colleges fielded their first football teams in the 1880s and 1890s. But by 1900, the sport was in crisis. Football was a violent game, and multiple players died because of in-game injuries.

In the early 1900s, officials considered banning the game altogether.

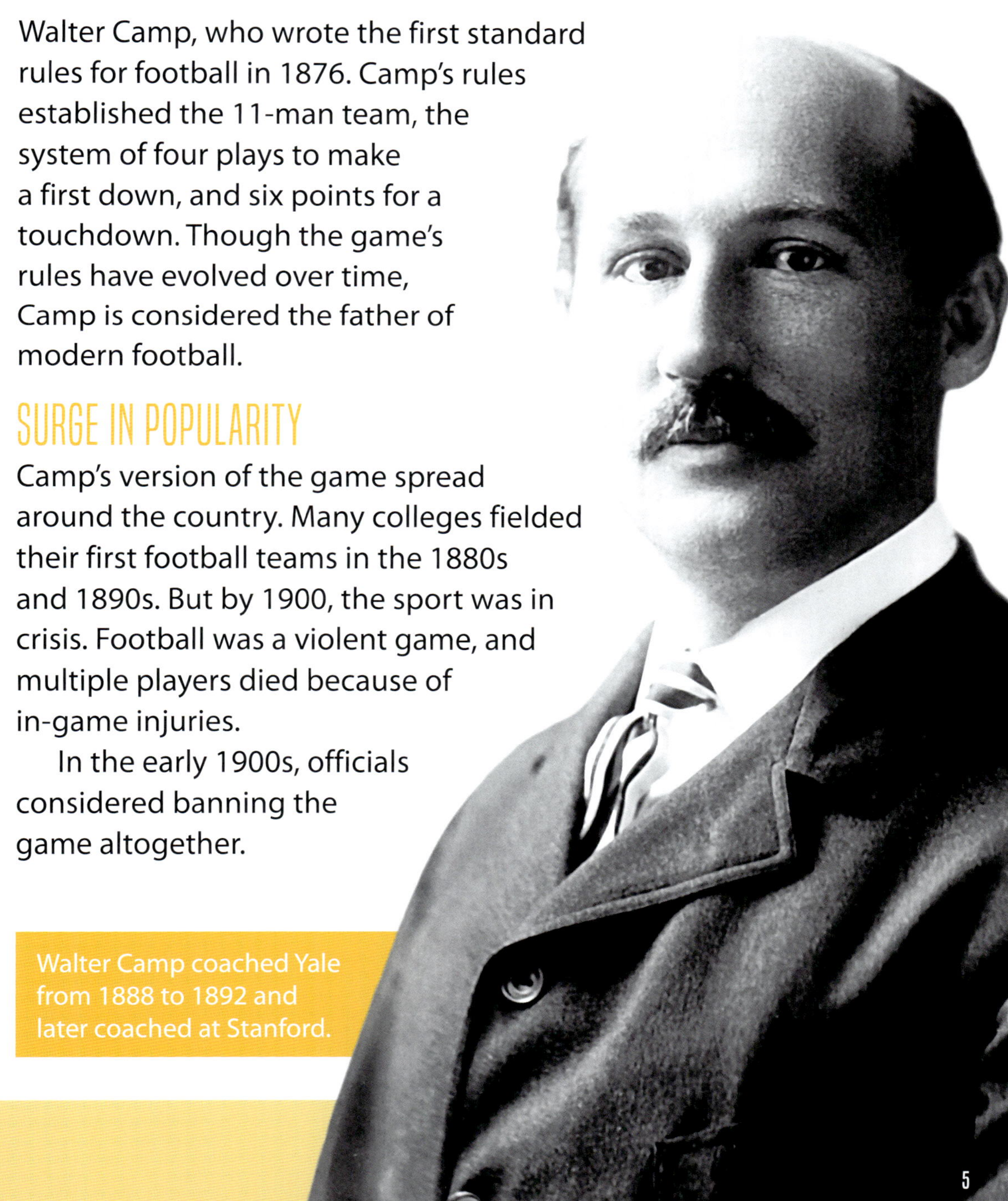

Walter Camp coached Yale from 1888 to 1892 and later coached at Stanford.

Jim Thorpe was one of college football's first great stars. He played at the Carlisle Indian Industrial School in Pennsylvania from 1907 to 1908, and 1911 to 1912.

Army takes on Notre Dame during a 1922 game in West Point, New York.

After President Theodore Roosevelt intervened, the Intercollegiate Athletic Association of the United States (IAAUS) was formed to regulate the game. The IAAUS eventually changed its name to the National Collegiate Athletic Association (NCAA). Among the changes the committee made were new rules that spread the players out along the field. The NCAA also developed safety pads and helmets.

The new, safer version of the game exploded nationwide. Professional football was in its infancy. The National Football League (NFL) wouldn't be founded until 1920. In the meantime, college football became more popular than ever. During the early 1900s, schools began pooling together into conferences. The initial versions of leagues such as the Big Ten, Southeastern Conference (SEC), and Big 12 were formed.

By the 1920s, players such as Illinois running back Red Grange were becoming national celebrities. Fans who wanted more football were treated to postseason bowl games. The Rose Bowl was first played in 1902. It became an annual tradition beginning in 1916. The Orange Bowl, Sugar Bowl, Sun Bowl, and Cotton Bowl were all founded between 1935 and 1937.

Cal's Roy Riegels races down the field against Georgia Tech in the Rose Bowl on January 1, 1929.

The University of Chicago's Jay Berwanger poses with the first Heisman Trophy in 1935. Nicknamed "The One-Man Team," he starred on offense, defense, and special teams.

In 1935, the Downtown Athletic Club of New York City decided to create an award to honor the best player in the nation. The first award was given to the do-it-all star Jay Berwanger of the University of Chicago. A year later, legendary coach John Heisman passed away. The innovative Heisman had modernized formations and the passing game while coaching at several schools, including Auburn, Clemson, and Georgia Tech. The Downtown Athletic Club renamed its award the Heisman Trophy.

WHO'S NO. 1?

In the first half of the 1900s, many different media outlets ranked football teams. At the end of the year, each picked its own national champion. Often, those champions differed. For some seasons, the NCAA recognizes as many as four national champions. In addition, many schools claim national titles from certain media outlets that are not recognized by the NCAA.

USC quarterback Vince Evans, *center*, scrambles to get away from pressure during a 1976 game against Notre Dame.

TRADITIONAL POWERS

By the 1950s, some of the early Ivy League powers had given way to larger schools. Big-time programs such as Notre Dame, Oklahoma, Ohio State, and Alabama dominated the game. And for the first time, college football was regularly shown on television. As big schools began receiving money from the broadcast television networks, the smaller schools struggled to compete.

In the 1960s, the top level of college football began to split in half. By 1973, the biggest schools made up Division I-A football, which eventually became known as the Football Bowl Subdivision (FBS). Smaller schools competed in Division I-AA, which would become the Football Championship Subdivision (FCS).

Traditional powers Alabama, Notre Dame, Oklahoma, and the University of Southern California (USC) all won national championships during the 1970s. However, there was no national title game. Instead, various polling systems were used to determine a national champion. In many seasons, different polls selected different winners. While some coaches began calling for a playoff system to determine a sole winner, debating the national champion became an annual tradition for college football fans.

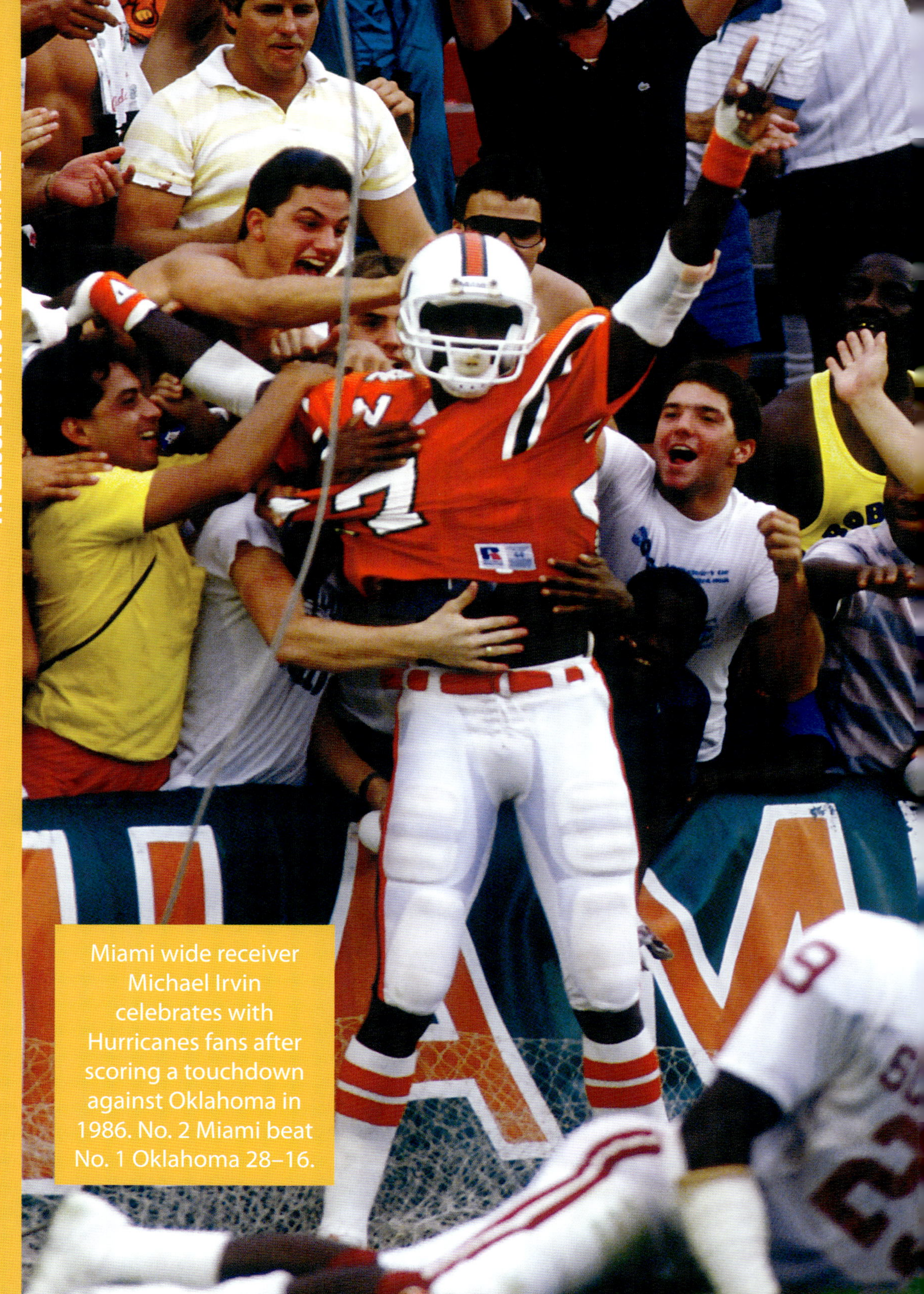

Miami wide receiver Michael Irvin celebrates with Hurricanes fans after scoring a touchdown against Oklahoma in 1986. No. 2 Miami beat No. 1 Oklahoma 28–16.

A CRAZY FINISH

College football games are famous for incredible game-winning plays. One of the most memorable came in 1982 between rivals Stanford and the University of California, Berkeley (Cal). Stanford scored a field goal with seconds left to go up 20–19. Time ran out on the next kickoff. But Cal kept the ball alive with a series of laterals. Thinking the game was over, the Stanford band filed out onto the field. But Cal's Kevin Moen eventually crossed over the goal line. He knocked over a trombone player as he scored the winning touchdown in a 25–20 Cal victory.

BIG BUSINESS

The 1980s brought many changes to the college football landscape. In Florida, the University of Miami and Florida State used the state's rich pipeline of talented high school players to build powerful programs. And while teams still longed to play in the most iconic bowl games, the number of postseason games increased from eight to 15.

With more bowl games and more television money, college football had become a big business. This made the desire to win even greater, and many schools were caught giving players benefits that were against NCAA rules. While recruiting scandals had been around since the beginning of college football, they were now a much bigger deal, and the NCAA was forced to dole out big punishments.

The most notorious of these situations came out of Southern Methodist University (SMU) in 1986. The Mustangs were a powerful team in the early part of the decade,

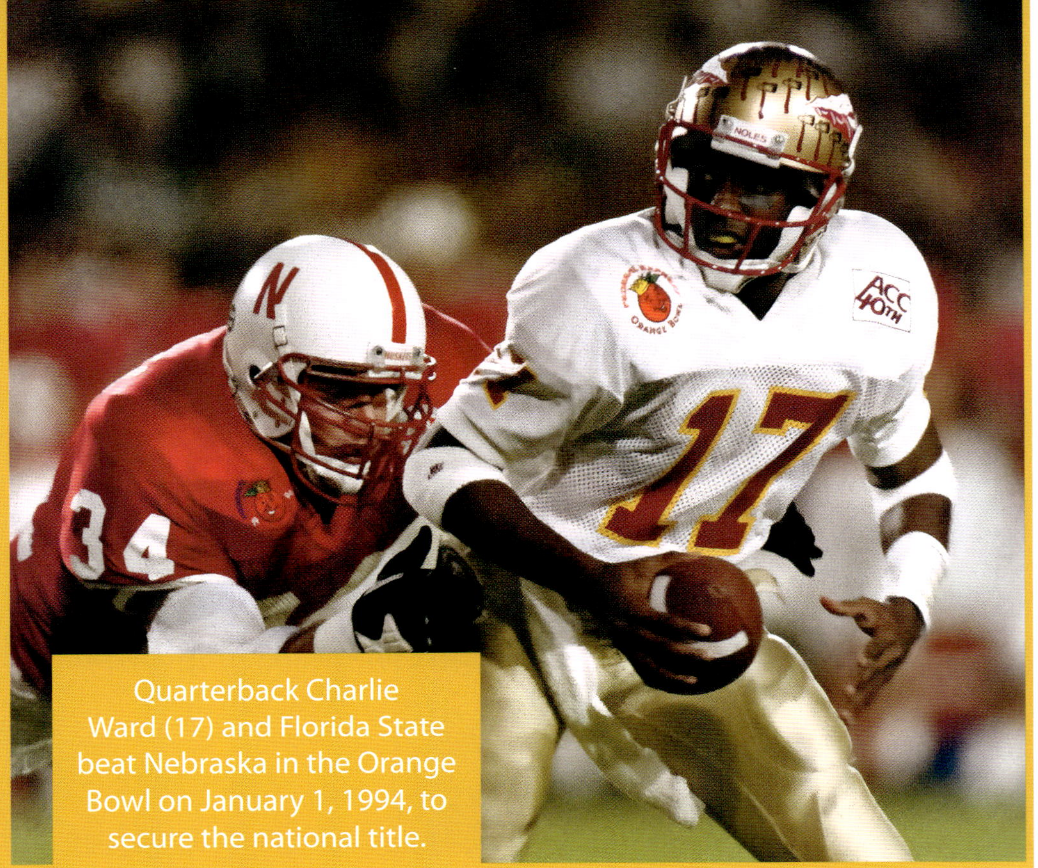

Quarterback Charlie Ward (17) and Florida State beat Nebraska in the Orange Bowl on January 1, 1994, to secure the national title.

competing in the Southwest Conference with schools such as Oklahoma, Texas, and Texas A&M. But supporters of SMU's program were paying out so many illegal benefits that the NCAA decided to shut down the program for two seasons. The so-called "death penalty" shocked college football.

CROWNING A CHAMPION

As the sport entered the 1990s, conferences remained locked into traditional partnerships with specific bowl games. For example, the Pac-10 champion met the Big Ten winner in the Rose Bowl. The Big 8 winner played in the Orange Bowl. The SEC champion went to the Sugar Bowl. These games, traditionally played on New Year's Day, could result in a thrilling end to the season. However, because of these bowl partnerships, often the two top-ranked teams didn't play each other.

In 1992, the Bowl Coalition was formed with the goal of creating a final matchup between the No. 1 and No. 2 teams. The coalition wasn't perfect, however, as the Rose Bowl refused to participate. Eventually, in 1998, Rose Bowl organizers came on board, and the Bowl Championship Series (BCS) was created. Now the top-ranked teams would always meet in a bowl game. However, fans still didn't love the system.

Michigan players celebrate after scoring a touchdown against Washington State in the Rose Bowl on January 1, 1998.

USC quarterback Matt Leinart led the Trojans to national titles in the 2003 and 2004 seasons.

The BCS used a computer system to rank the teams. Its decisions often created controversies. Schools from less-powerful conferences with undefeated records were often left out. Having a single championship game also led to issues. In 2003, Louisiana State University (LSU), Oklahoma, and USC all finished the regular season with one loss. The BCS paired LSU against Oklahoma in the title game, while USC went to the Rose Bowl. When LSU and USC both won their games, each team claimed the national title.

BOWL EXPLOSION

Throughout the 1990s and 2000s, the number of postseason bowl games grew dramatically. In 1990, there were 19 bowl games. By 2024, that number had grown to 47. That meant more than half of the 134 FBS teams reached a postseason game.

A year later, Auburn, Oklahoma, USC, and Utah all went into their bowl games undefeated. USC defeated Oklahoma in the BCS title game, but both Auburn and Utah won bowl games too. With three undefeated teams at the end of the year, fans once again debated who was really the champion.

To finally fix the problem, the NCAA debuted the first four-team College Football Playoff in 2014. The winners of two semifinal games met for the national title, and a single champion was crowned. The tournament expanded to 12 teams for the 2024 season.

By that point, the college football world had changed dramatically. Court rulings in 2020 paved the way for athletes to earn money on their name, image, and likeness (NIL).

Schools scrambled to secure big-money deals for the best players. The first 12-team playoff champion, Ohio State, reportedly spent $20 million to build its talented roster.

Schools have long switched conferences. But during the 2010s and early 2020s, conference realignment went to a new level. Many schools abandoned traditional rivalries and nearby opponents in favor of more money in different conferences.

Alabama quarterback Jalen Milroe scrambles against Georgia during the 2023 SEC Championship Game. Alabama beat Georgia 27–24.

Ohio State linebacker Jack Sawyer celebrates after the team won the first 12-team College Football Playoff in January 2025.

By the start of the 2024 season, the Big Ten had 18 teams. The Big 12 and the SEC had 16 each. The Pac-12, which had existed since 1915, broke up as teams moved to new conferences. Two schools from California, Cal and Stanford, ended up in the Atlantic Coast Conference (ACC).

Still, fans flocked to college football. Despite the changes, the tradition of watching many old rivalries continued. Fans kept packing stadiums, and the sport remained one of the most popular attractions in the United States.

ALABAMA CRIMSON TIDE

Football was first played at Alabama in 1892. And though the school had consistently great teams for decades, it wasn't until coach Paul "Bear" Bryant arrived in 1958 that Alabama became truly elite. The hard-nosed Bryant was famous for his houndstooth fedora and his legendary rugged practices. But those difficult days on the practice field made Alabama a consistent champion.

Before Bryant's retirement in 1983, his teams won or shared six national titles. The team's most dramatic win came in the Sugar Bowl after the 1978 season. Alabama's fourth-quarter goal-line stand against Penn State secured a 14–7 win and a national crown.

Nearly three decades after Bryant left, Alabama's second great coach arrived on campus. Nick Saban took over a struggling team in 2007 and quickly turned things around. Alabama became the country's premier program for the next 15 years. In that time, Saban

Coach Bear Bryant won a then-record 323 victories in his career, including 232 while at Alabama.

delivered another six national titles. The most memorable win came after the 2017 season. Quarterback Tua Tagovailoa threw a 41-yard overtime touchdown pass to receiver DeVonta Smith that secured a come-from-behind 26–23 win over rival Georgia in the College Football Playoff.

Not surprisingly, Alabama has fielded some of the greatest players ever. Receiver Don Hutson helped revolutionize the passing game in the 1930s. Flashy quarterback Joe Namath

Wide receiver DeVonta Smith hauls in his game-winning touchdown against Georgia in the BCS National Championship Game on January 8, 2018.

led the Crimson Tide to the national title in 1964 with his pinpoint passes. Menacing linebacker Derrick Thomas racked up 27 sacks in 1988. That's considered an unofficial NCAA record. It is unofficial because sack statistics weren't officially recorded until 2000.

BECOMING THE TIDE

Alabama can trace its unusual nickname back to the program's early days. At first, the team was called "The Cadets." But after playing Auburn on a muddy field in 1907, the team's white uniforms were stained red. A sportswriter dubbed the team the Crimson Tide, and the nickname stuck.

An Alabama fan holds up a sign with the school's signature "Roll Tide" slogan.

Despite the school's many stars, Alabama didn't produce a Heisman Trophy winner until 2009. That year, Tide running back Mark Ingram took home the prestigious award. Three more Alabama winners soon followed. Running back Derrick Henry captured the 2015 award. Wide receiver DeVonta Smith won in 2020. One year later, Bryce Young became the first Alabama quarterback to win the award.

FACT BOX

First Season: 1892

Location: Tuscaloosa, Alabama

Stadium: Bryant-Denny Stadium

Conference: Southeastern Conference

All-Time Record: 974–341–43

Bowl Record: 42–26–3

National Titles: 1925, 1926, 1930, *1934,** *1941,** *1961*, *1964*, *1965*, *1973*, *1978*, 1979, 1992, 2009, 2011, 2012, 2015, 2017, 2020

College Football Playoff Appearances: 2014, 2015, 2016, 2017, 2018, 2020, 2021, 2023

Top Coaches: Frank Thomas (1931–46); Paul "Bear" Bryant (1958–82); Nick Saban (2007–23)

Top Players: Don Hutson (1932–34); Joe Namath (1962–64); Derrick Thomas (1986–88); Mark Ingram (2008–10); Derrick Henry (2013–15); DeVonta Smith (2017–20); Bryce Young (2020–22)

Mascot: Big Al

*Title claimed by school, though not recognized by the NCAA.

Shared National Titles in Italics

ARIZONA STATE SUN DEVILS

The school that would become Arizona State University began playing football in 1897. At the time, Arizona had yet to become a state. The Owls, as the team was known, represented the Territorial Normal School.

After changing its nickname to the Bulldogs, the school by then called Arizona State Teachers College reached the Sun Bowl twice in the late 1930s. In 1945, the university shortened its name to Arizona State. A year later, students led a movement to change the nickname again. The team has been known as the Sun Devils ever since.

While Arizona State has enjoyed consistent success over the years, truly great

Sparky, the mascot of the Arizona State Sun Devils, was first drawn by former Disney artist Berk Anthony.

seasons have been less common. In 1970, legendary coach Frank Kush led the team to an 11–0 record, which included the school's first bowl victory. The Sun Devils routed North Carolina 48–26 in the Peach Bowl. Five years later, Kush led an 11–0 Arizona State team into a Fiesta Bowl matchup against powerhouse Nebraska. The Sun Devils won 17–14 on a late field goal by Kush's son, Danny. Arizona State finished the season ranked No. 2 behind national champion Oklahoma.

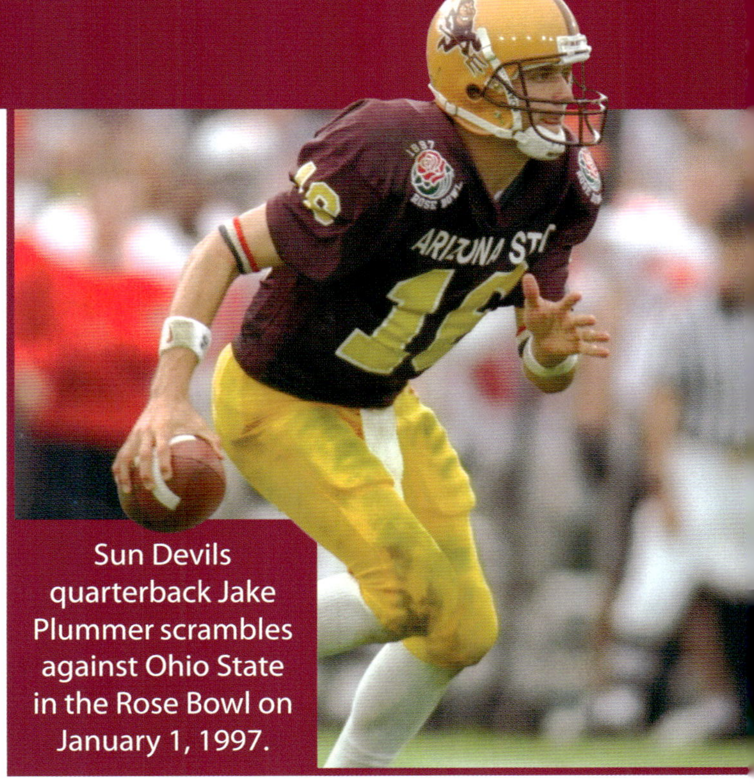

Sun Devils quarterback Jake Plummer scrambles against Ohio State in the Rose Bowl on January 1, 1997.

After joining the Pac-10 in 1978, the Sun Devils earned the conference's Rose Bowl bid twice. The first came after the 1986 season, when Arizona State knocked off Michigan 22–15 in the prestigious bowl game. Star quarterback Jake Plummer led the Sun Devils back to the Rose Bowl after the 1996 season with an 11–0 record. The team could have secured a share of the national title by beating Ohio State. Instead, the Sun Devils fell 20–17 on a Buckeyes touchdown in the final minute.

Arizona State fans waited nearly three decades for the team to challenge for the national title again. That finally came after the school joined the Big 12 in 2024. Behind record-setting running back Cam Skattebo, the Sun Devils charged to a conference title. That earned Arizona State a spot in the College Football Playoff. Facing Texas in the Peach Bowl, Skattebo rushed for 143 yards and two touchdowns, caught eight passes for 99 yards, and threw a touchdown pass. Despite Skattebo's heroics, Arizona State lost 39–31 in double overtime.

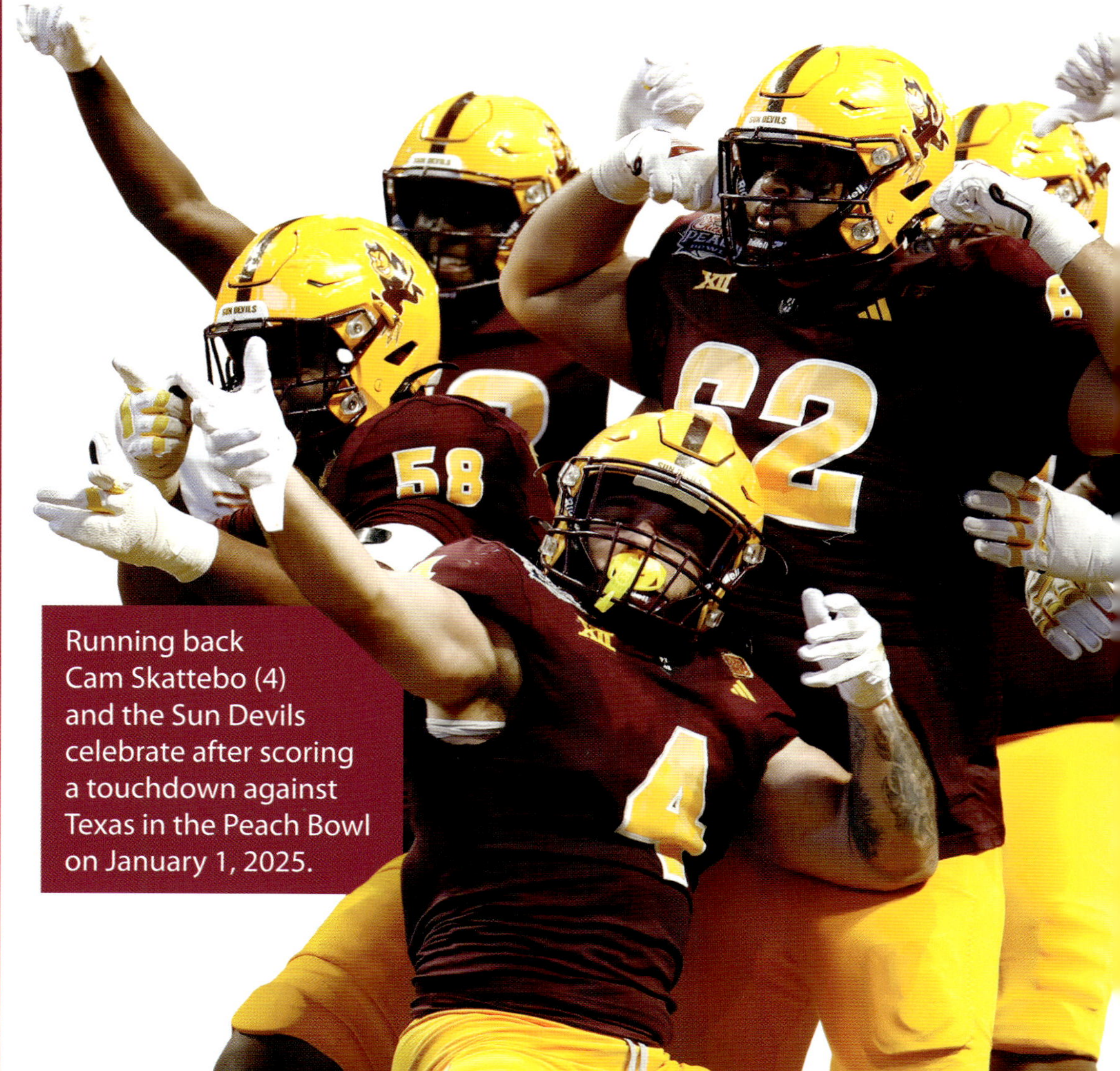

Running back Cam Skattebo (4) and the Sun Devils celebrate after scoring a touchdown against Texas in the Peach Bowl on January 1, 2025.

PAT TILLMAN

Linebacker Pat Tillman starred at Arizona State from 1994 to 1997. He then joined the NFL's Arizona Cardinals. After the terrorist attacks of September 11, 2001, Tillman gave up his football career and joined the US Army Rangers. Tillman was killed in 2004 while serving in Afghanistan. The university founded the Pat Tillman Veterans Center in 2011. The center counsels students who are also in the military.

FACT BOX

First Season: 1897

Location: Tempe, Arizona

Stadium: Mountain America Stadium

Conference: Big 12 Conference

All-Time Record: 649–427–24

Bowl Record: 15–18–1

National Titles: None

College Football Playoff Appearances: 2024

Top Coaches: Frank Kush (1958–79); Darryl Rogers (1980–84); Bruce Snyder (1992–2000)

Top Players: Wilford "Whizzer" White (1947–50); Danny White (1971–73); Woody Green (1971–73); Mike Richardson (1979–82); David Fulcher (1983–85); Randall McDaniel (1984–87); Jake Plummer (1993–96); Terrell Suggs (2000–02); Cam Skattebo (2023–24)

Mascot: Sparky the Sun Devil

AUBURN TIGERS

Auburn fans salute the "War Eagle" as it flies through Jordan-Hare Stadium. The eagle has been part of Auburn football history since the program was founded in 1892.

Located "on the plains" in eastern Alabama, Auburn forms half of one of college football's fiercest rivalries with the neighboring University of Alabama. Their annual game, known as the Iron Bowl, is typically played on the last Saturday of the season. It has been so heated through the years that the schools refused to play each other from 1907 to 1948.

Auburn has enjoyed periods of great success over the years. Legendary coach Ralph Jordan led the team to a perfect 10–0 record in 1957. The Tigers allowed only 28 points all season. Though Auburn was on probation and not allowed to play in a bowl game, the Associated Press awarded the school its first widely recognized national championship.

In 1971, Auburn quarterback Pat Sullivan led the nation with 20 touchdown passes on the way to becoming the school's first Heisman Trophy winner. Running back Bo Jackson won Auburn's second Heisman in 1985. Jackson was such a gifted athlete that he eventually played both football and baseball professionally. During his Heisman season, Jackson rushed for 1,786 yards, which remained a school record until 2013. But his most famous play came three years earlier in the 1982 Iron Bowl. With Auburn trailing late, Jackson showed his skills as a former state champion high jumper when he leaped over the pile to score a touchdown. Auburn held on to win 23–22,

Running back Bo Jackson rushed for a school-record 4,303 yards during his career at Auburn from 1982 to 1985.

TOOMER'S CORNER

After big wins, Auburn fans meet outside Toomer's Drugs on Magnolia Avenue and College Street. They celebrate by "rolling" the trees, statues, light poles, and any other non-moving objects with toilet paper. In 2013, an Alabama fan poisoned the famous oak trees at Toomer's Corner. The dead trees were removed. Auburn students planted new trees to carry on the tradition.

Quarterback Cam Newton runs away from Alabama defenders during the 2010 Iron Bowl.

ending a nine-game losing streak against the Crimson Tide. The play is remembered by Auburn fans as "Bo Over the Top."

The Tigers broke through for another national title during the 2010 season. Led by Heisman Trophy–winning dual-threat quarterback Cam Newton, Auburn finished 12–0 in the regular season. The Tigers rallied from a 24–0 deficit against Alabama to win the Iron Bowl 28–27. Auburn then finished off its perfect season by beating Oregon 22–19 in the BCS National Championship Game.

FACT BOX

First Season: 1892

Location: Auburn, Alabama

Stadium: Jordan-Hare Stadium

Conference: Southeastern Conference

All-Time Record: 804–478–47

Bowl Record: 23–20–2

National Titles: *1910,* * *1913, 1914,* * *1957, 1958,* * *1983, 1993, 2004,* * 2010

College Football Playoff Appearances: None

Top Coaches: Mike Donahue (1904–22); Ralph Jordan (1951–75); Pat Dye (1981–92)

Top Players: Ken Rice (1957–60); Terry Beasley (1969–71); Pat Sullivan (1969–71); James Brooks (1977–80); Bo Jackson (1982–85); Tracy Rocker (1985–88); Cadillac Williams (2001–04); Cam Newton (2010)

Mascot: Aubie the Tiger

*Title claimed by school, though not recognized by the NCAA.

Shared National Titles in Italics

The crowd's loud reaction registered on a seismometer, which is usually used to measure earthquakes.

"The Kick Six" was the only touchdown Chris Davis scored in his Auburn career.

THE KICK SIX

- **The Setup**
  Alabama visited Auburn's Jordan-Hare Stadium for the 2013 Iron Bowl. The two-time defending champion Crimson Tide were undefeated and ranked No. 1. Auburn was ranked No. 4 with a 10–1 record.
- **The Play**
  Auburn tied the game 28–28 with 32 seconds left. But Alabama still had time. With one second remaining, kicker Adam Griffith lined up for a 57-yard field goal. It came up short. Instead, Auburn cornerback Chris Davis caught the ball nine yards deep in his own end zone. He then raced untouched down the left sideline for a 109-yard touchdown. Auburn won the game 34–28.
- **The Legacy**
  In 2015, fans voted "The Kick Six" the greatest college football play of all time.

BOISE STATE BRONCOS

Boise State was still a junior college when its first football team took the field in 1933. Over the next six decades, the school changed to a four-year institution and became a Division I-AA (now known as FCS) powerhouse. The Broncos moved up to the FBS level in 1996.

Originally, the school was best known for the signature blue turf at its home stadium. But the Broncos soon earned a reputation for winning football games. Playing in the smaller Big West Conference, Boise State had its first winning FBS season in 1998. Through 2024, the school had not had a losing record since.

Now called Albertsons Stadium, Boise State's home field has featured blue turf since 1986.

Boise State running back Ian Johnson, *right*, scores the winning two-point conversion against Oklahoma in the Fiesta Bowl on January 1, 2007.

Boise State was still considered an underdog program when it went 12–0 in 2006 and earned an invite to the Fiesta Bowl. Facing heavy favorite Oklahoma, the Broncos pulled off one of the biggest upsets in college football history. After trailing 28–10 in the first half, Boise State used a series of trick plays to tie the game 35–35 and force overtime. The Broncos then won 43–42 on a two-point conversion run from tailback Ian Johnson.

Boise State proved its success was no fluke by winning the Fiesta Bowl after the 2009 and

UNIFORM BAN

When Boise State joined the Mountain West Conference in 2009, the conference had an unusual demand. Officials banned Boise State from wearing blue uniforms for home games. The league said that the blue uniforms gave Boise State an advantage when they blended in with the school's blue field. The ban lasted for two seasons before it was lifted.

Broncos running back Ashton Jeanty rushed for 2,601 yards in 2024. That was just 28 yards short of the NCAA record for a single season.

2014 seasons. The Broncos later took another big step when they reached the College Football Playoff in 2024. Led by Heisman Trophy runner-up running back Ashton Jeanty, Boise State entered the playoff with a 12–1 record before being knocked out by Penn State in the quarterfinals. It was Boise State's 19th season with at least 10 wins since joining the FBS. In that span, the Broncos had the highest winning percentage of any top-level program.

FACT BOX

First Season: 1968

Location: Boise, Idaho

Stadium: Albertsons Stadium

Conference: Mountain West Conference

All-Time FBS Record: 502–189–2

Bowl Record: 13–8

National Titles: None

College Football Playoff Appearances: 2024

Top Coaches: Dan Hawkins (2001–05); Chris Petersen (2006–13); Bryan Harsin (2014–20)

Top Players: Randy Trautman (1978–81); Ian Johnson (2005–08); Austin Pettis (2007–10); Kellen Moore (2008–11); Leighton Vander Esch (2014–17); Brett Rypien (2015–18); Ashton Jeanty (2022–24)

Mascot: Buster Bronco

BYU COUGARS

Brigham Young University, also known as BYU, is unique among major college football programs. The school is affiliated with the Church of Jesus Christ of Latter-day Saints, also known as the Mormons. Though not all players who suit up for the Cougars are Mormon, all students at BYU must live by the school's strict honor code.

Although those limits sometimes make it harder for BYU to recruit new players, the football team has been strong since the early 1970s. Coach LaVell Edwards brought his pioneering passing attack to Provo, Utah, in 1972, 50 years after the school started fielding a team. In 1974, Edwards led the Cougars to their first bowl game.

BYU's first bowl win came after the 1980 season. The Cougars trailed SMU 45–25

LaVell Edwards coached Brigham Young from 1972 to 2000 and had only one losing season.

BYU's LaVell Edwards Stadium sits at the foot of the Wasatch Mountains.

with just over four minutes remaining in the Holiday Bowl. Quarterback Jim McMahon led a thrilling comeback. Aided by an onside kick recovery and a blocked punt, BYU scored three touchdowns. The last was a Hail Mary on the final play to win 46–45. The game was called "The Miracle Bowl" by Cougars fans.

Four years later, BYU captured its only national title. The Cougars finished the regular season 12–0 and won the

Western Athletic Conference. They then beat Michigan in the Holiday Bowl to wrap up a perfect season. More than 40 years later, BYU was still the last team from outside one of the biggest conferences to win a national championship.

Because Edwards's offense featured the passing game, quarterbacks flocked to

Quarterback Ty Detmer threw for more than 15,000 yards in his four seasons at BYU from 1988 to 1991.

CONFERENCE HOPPING

BYU has played in six conferences since the program was founded. BYU also played as an independent program from 2011 to 2022. After the 2022 season, the Cougars joined the Big 12. It was the first time in program history the school had joined a major conference.

BYU in the 1970s, 1980s, and 1990s. Marc Wilson, McMahon, Steve Young, and Ty Detmer all put up huge numbers before going on to NFL careers. Football observers referred to the school as "Quarterback U." Detmer became the first Cougar to win the Heisman Trophy. He took home the award in 1990 after throwing for 5,188 yards and 41 touchdowns.

FACT BOX

First Season: 1922

Location: Provo, Utah

Stadium: LaVell Edwards Stadium

Conference: Big 12 Conference

All-Time Record: 627–445–26

Bowl Record: 18–22–1

National Titles: 1984

College Football Playoff Appearances: None

Top Coaches: LaVell Edwards (1972–2000); Bronco Mendenhall (2005–15); Kalani Sitake (2016–)

Top Players: Marion Probert (1951–54); Gifford Nielsen (1975–77); Marc Wilson (1977–79); Jim McMahon (1977–81); Gordon Hudson (1981–83); Steve Young (1981–83); Robbie Bosco (1983–85); Ty Detmer (1988–91); Luke Staley (1999–2001)

Mascot: Cosmo the Cougar

CLEMSON TIGERS

Quarterback Trevor Lawrence celebrates a Clemson touchdown against Alabama in the National Championship Game in January 2019.

The Clemson Tigers first became a national power in the late 1930s and early 1940s. Much of their early success came under legendary coach Frank Howard. In his 30 seasons before retiring in 1969, Howard led Clemson to six bowl games and two undefeated seasons. The school renamed the field at Memorial Stadium as Frank Howard Field in 1974.

Despite that success, Clemson didn't win its first national title until 1981. After finishing just 6–5 in 1980, the Tigers were not considered a contender before the next season started. But 33-year-old coach Danny Ford led Clemson to a 12–0 record. The Tigers were a dominant defensive team. They allowed only 7.5 points per game and forced a school-record 43 turnovers. Clemson capped off the

Clemson players touch Howard's Rock as they enter the field before a game in 2019.

HOWARD'S ROCK

Clemson football players enter every game by walking down a hill at Memorial Stadium's east end zone. There, they pass Howard's Rock. The rock came from Death Valley, California. It was given to coach Frank Howard as a gift. Before a 1966 game, an assistant placed it on a pedestal. When Clemson won, the rock became a good-luck charm. Players began touching Howard's Rock before entering the field in 1967. That tradition remains to this day.

year by upsetting favored Nebraska 22–15 in the Orange Bowl to finish as the nation's only undefeated team.

Though Clemson remained a strong team throughout the 1980s, 1990s, and 2000s, it didn't climb back to the top of the college football mountain until the 2010s. Under coach Dabo Swinney, the Tigers challenged Alabama as the top team in the country for several seasons in the new College Football Playoff format. The schools' first meeting in the title game came after the 2015 season. Alabama won a 45–40 thriller.

FACT BOX

First Season: 1896

Location: Clemson, South Carolina

Stadium: Memorial Stadium

Conference: Atlantic Coast Conference

All-Time Record: 808–476–45

Bowl Record: 27–24

National Titles: 1981, 2016, 2018

College Football Playoff Appearances: 2015, 2016, 2017, 2018, 2019, 2020, 2024

Top Coaches: Frank Howard (1940–69); Danny Ford (1978–89); Dabo Swinney (2008–)

Top Players: Banks McFadden (1937–39); Steve Fuller (1975–78); Terry Kinard (1979–82); C. J. Spiller (2006–09); DeAndre Hopkins (2010–12); Vic Beasley (2011–14); Deshaun Watson (2014–16); Trevor Lawrence (2018–20)

Mascot: The Tiger

Clemson avenged the loss a year later. Quarterback Deshaun Watson's two-yard touchdown pass to Hunter Renfrow on the game's final play gave Clemson a 35–31 victory and a national title. The Tigers met the Crimson Tide in the title game again after the 2018 season. Led by standout freshman quarterback Trevor Lawrence, Clemson routed Alabama 44–16 for a third championship.

Clemson's biggest rival remains in-state foe South Carolina. The two schools traditionally meet on the field in the Palmetto Bowl. The game was first played in 1896. The teams met every year from 1909 to 2019. Clemson won the matchup for the 73rd time in 2023.

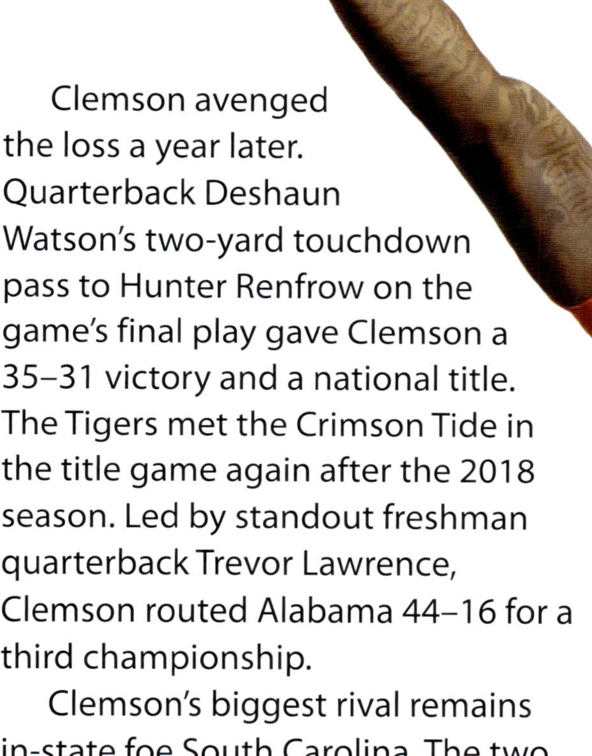

Clemson wide receiver Tee Higgins points for a first down in the 2017 Palmetto Bowl. Clemson won the game 34–10.

COLORADO BUFFALOES

The Colorado Buffaloes began playing as an independent team in 1890. The program had its first taste of success in the early 1900s under Fred Folsom. The coach led Colorado to three undefeated seasons in a row between 1909 and 1911.

After 28 seasons in the Rocky Mountain Athletic Conference, and then another ten in the Mountain States Athletic Conference, the Buffaloes joined the Big 7 Conference in 1948. It would eventually become the Big 8 and later the Big 12. No matter the size, Colorado won the conference only five times before leaving to join the Pac-12 in 2011.

The Buffaloes enjoyed their most successful period under popular coach Bill McCartney. He took over a struggling

A team of handlers leads Ralphie VI, Colorado's live mascot, onto Folsom Field before a 2024 game.

Colorado coach Bill McCartney, *left*, celebrates with a member of his staff after the Buffaloes' 10–9 win over Notre Dame in the Orange Bowl on January 1, 1991.

program in 1982 and slowly built Colorado into a national power. The team's peak came in 1990. Despite winning only one of their first three games that season, the Buffaloes finished 11–1–1 while playing one of the toughest schedules in the country. Colorado played seven top-25 teams. The Buffaloes capped the year with a 10–9 win over No. 5 Notre Dame in the Orange Bowl. The Associated Press, which ran one of the two major polls at the time, voted Colorado the national champion.

Colorado continued its success through the early 2000s under coaches Rick Neuheisel and Gary Barnett. But starting in 2006, the Buffaloes began to struggle. They reached only three bowl games in 18 years.

In 2023, the school hired flashy coach Deion Sanders. A former superstar player, Sanders attracted top recruits. Many stars also transferred to Colorado. One of the biggest was wide receiver/defensive back Travis Hunter. In 2024, he became the school's second Heisman Trophy winner. Running back Rashaan Salaam was the first in 1994. Colorado also rejoined the Big 12 in 2024 and registered just its third winning season since 2010.

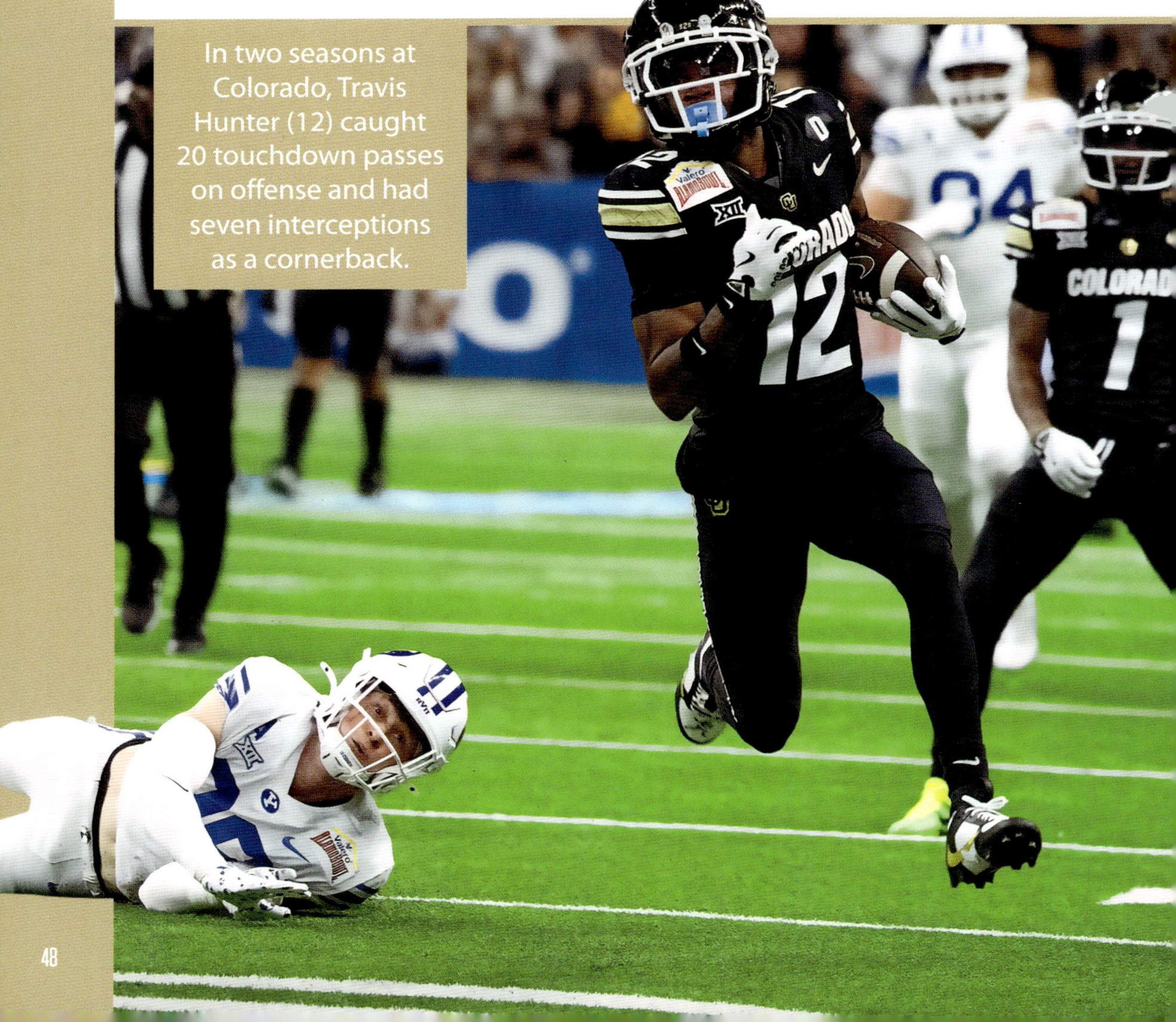

In two seasons at Colorado, Travis Hunter (12) caught 20 touchdown passes on offense and had seven interceptions as a cornerback.

THE FIFTH DOWN

Facing Missouri in 1990, Colorado benefited from one of the biggest refereeing mistakes ever made. On a key series near the Missouri goal line, the Buffaloes were accidentally given five downs. Colorado scored on the fifth play and won the game 33–31. The Buffaloes eventually went on to claim a share of the national title that season.

FACT BOX

First Season: 1890

Location: Boulder, Colorado

Stadium: Folsom Field

Conference: Big 12 Conference

All-Time Record: 732–548–36

Bowl Record: 12–19

National Titles: *1990*

College Football Playoff Appearances: None

Top Coaches: Fred Folsom (1902, 1908–15); Bill McCartney (1982–94); Rick Neuheisel (1995–98)

Top Players: Banks McFadden (1937–39); Byron White (1935–37); Joe Romig (1959–61); Bobby Anderson (1967–69); Eric Bieniemy (1987–90); Jay Leeuwenburg (1989–91); Rashaan Salaam (1992–94); Travis Hunter (2023–24)

Mascot: Ralphie the Buffalo

Shared National Titles in Italics

FLORIDA GATORS

Florida's football program was founded in 1906, but the school did not field a consistently successful team for nearly 60 years. Coach Ray Graves led the Gators to four bowl victories between 1960 and 1969. Graves's most celebrated team won the Orange Bowl after the 1966 season. That team was led by Heisman Trophy–winning quarterback Steve Spurrier.

After struggling in the 1970s, the Gators got back to winning in the 1980s under coaches Charley Pell and Galen Hall.

Steve Spurrier was a Heisman Trophy–winning quarterback before coaching the Gators to a national title. The University of Florida named the field at Ben Hill Griffin Stadium after him in 2016.

Florida quarterback Danny Wuerffel throws a pass against Florida State in the Sugar Bowl on January 2, 1997.

But it wasn't until Spurrier returned as coach in 1990 that Florida became a major contender. Behind his entertaining pass-oriented offense, Spurrier led the Gators to at least nine wins in each of his 12 seasons in charge.

That run included a 12–1 record in 1996. Quarterback Danny Wuerffel led all FBS passers with 39 touchdowns that year. He became the school's first Heisman Trophy winner since Spurrier three decades earlier. The Gators finished the season by routing rival Florida State 52–20 in the Sugar Bowl. After the game, Florida was named the national champion.

A decade later, second-year coach Urban Meyer led Florida to a second title. The Gators finished 13–1 behind a sturdy defense. They finished the season with a 41–14 rout of Ohio State in the BCS Championship Game.

In 2008, Meyer's team piled up 611 points in 14 games. The Gators finished 13–1 again, this time with 2007 Heisman winner Tim Tebow under center. The dual-threat Tebow tossed a pair of touchdowns in a 24–14 win over Oklahoma to deliver the school's second title in three seasons.

Gators quarterback Tim Tebow threw 32 touchdown passes and ran for 23 more on his way to winning the Heisman Trophy in 2007.

THIRST QUENCHING

In 1965, University of Florida scientist Dr. James Robert Cade was studying the effect of electrolytes on athletes. He developed a sports drink that could help Florida's football players refuel on hot days. The team first used the drink in a victory over LSU when the temperature was 102 degrees Fahrenheit (39°C). Cade's beverage was a hit, and soon it was sold as Gatorade. It is still the most popular sports drink in the United States.

FACT BOX

First Season: 1906

Location: Gainesville, Florida

Stadium: Ben Hill Griffin Stadium

Conference: Southeastern Conference

All-Time Record: 766–450–40

Bowl Record: 25–24

National Titles: 1996, 2006, 2008

College Football Playoff Appearances: None

Top Coaches: Ray Graves (1960–69); Steve Spurrier (1990–2001); Urban Meyer (2005–10)

Top Players: Steve Spurrier (1964–66); Jack Youngblood (1968–70); Wes Chandler (1974–77); Wilber Marshall (1980–83); Emmitt Smith (1987–89); Danny Wuerffel (1993–96); Tim Tebow (2006–09)

Mascot: Albert and Alberta Gator

FLORIDA STATE SEMINOLES

Florida State had mostly losing football teams until Bobby Bowden was hired to coach the team in 1976. Bowden went 5–6 in his first year. He then didn't have a losing season for the next three decades.

The Seminoles put together several impressive streaks under Bowden. Florida State went 13–0–1 in bowl games from

Florida State quarterback Charlie Ward (17) scrambles during the Orange Bowl after the 1993 season.

In 34 years coaching Florida State, Bobby Bowden led the Seminoles to 315 wins.

the 1982 to 1995 seasons. Bowden's teams won at least 10 games every year from 1987 to 2000. The team captured its first national championship after the 1993 season. Behind Heisman Trophy–winning quarterback Charlie Ward, Florida State went 12–1. After outscoring opponents by an average of 34 points during the season, the Seminoles squeaked out an 18–16 win over Nebraska in the Orange Bowl. Florida State won the game when the Cornhuskers' kicker missed a game-winning field-goal attempt on the final snap.

OSCEOLA AND RENEGADE

People of the Seminole Tribe have lived in what is now Florida for roughly 14,000 years. Florida State's nickname comes from Florida's ties to the Seminole Tribe. Before games, a man dressed as celebrated Seminole figure Osceola rides onto the field on a white Appaloosa horse named Renegade. Osceola's clothing was designed by members of the Seminole Tribe.

Florida State won its second national title in 1999 by routing Virginia Tech 46–29 in the Sugar Bowl. The victory capped Bowden's first perfect season as a head coach. The team slipped in the 2000s, however, and Bowden stepped down after the 2009 season.

Florida State wide receiver Kelvin Benjamin leaps to grab the winning touchdown late in the BCS National Championship Game in January 2014.

Bowden's replacement, Jimbo Fisher, quickly revived the program. In 2013, he guided Florida State to the national championship game with the help of star quarterback Jameis Winston. Winston became the first freshman to win the national title and the Heisman Trophy in the same season. The quarterback threw two touchdown passes in the BCS title game. The second, to receiver Kelvin Benjamin, came with 13 seconds left in the game to secure a 34–31 win over Auburn.

FACT BOX

First Season: 1947*

Location: Tallahassee, Florida

Stadium: Doak S. Campbell Stadium

Conference: Atlantic Coast Conference

All-Time Record: 583–291–17

Bowl Record: 32–16–2

National Titles: 1993, 1999, 2013

College Football Playoff Appearances: 2013

Top Coaches: Bill Peterson (1960–70); Bobby Bowden (1976–2009); Jimbo Fisher (2010–17)

Top Players: Ron Simmons (1977–80); Deion Sanders (1985–88); Charlie Ward (1989–94); Marvin Jones (1990–92); Derrick Brooks (1991–94); Peter Warrick (1995–99); Chris Weinke (1997–2000); Jameis Winston (2013–14)

Mascot: None

*The school also fielded a team from 1902 to 1904.

GEORGIA BULLDOGS

Georgia fullback Frank Sinkwich, *far right*, races through the UCLA defense for the only touchdown of the Rose Bowl on January 1, 1943.

The University of Georgia has been fielding successful football teams since the 1890s. The Bulldogs were a power in the Southern Conference in the early 1900s. They then helped form the SEC in 1933.

In 1942, Georgia put together its first championship season. Behind the offensive attack of Heisman Trophy–winning fullback Frank Sinkwich and tough halfback Charley Trippi, the Bulldogs went 10–1 in the regular season. Coach Wallace Butts's team then shut out UCLA 9–0 in the Rose Bowl. At the time, several news services named their own national champions. Georgia was selected by many of them. But the NCAA does not recognize Georgia as the season's champion.

There was no disputing the Bulldogs' success in 1980. Powered by nearly unstoppable freshman running back Herschel Walker, Georgia went into the Sugar Bowl on

Georgia running back Herschel Walker (34) won the Heisman Trophy after his junior season in 1982.

January 1, 1981, with an 11–0 record. Walker scored a pair of touchdowns to lead the Bulldogs to a 17–10 win over Notre Dame. Both major polls named coach Vince Dooley's team the national champion.

Polls weren't needed in the early 2020s. The NCAA had adopted the College Football Playoff system nearly a decade earlier. Georgia had reached the championship game after the 2017 season and lost a heartbreaking 26–23 overtime game to rival Alabama. After the 2021 season, the Bulldogs and Crimson Tide faced off again for the title. This time, Georgia quarterback

UGA

Georgia's live mascot is an English bulldog named Uga. He spends games in an air-conditioned doghouse inside Sanford Stadium. Many dogs have served as Uga since the mascot debuted in 1956. A dog named Boom took over as Uga XI in 2023. The dogs are bred by the Seiler family of Savannah, Georgia.

Bulldogs quarterback Stetson Bennett threw four touchdown passes and also ran for two scores in the National Championship Game win over Texas Christian in January 2023.

Stetson Bennett threw two second-half touchdowns to help the Bulldogs pull away 33–18.

Bennett and coach Kirby Smart led Georgia back to the playoffs after the 2022 season. The Bulldogs rallied from 14 points down in the fourth quarter to beat Ohio State in the semifinals. Georgia then capped off a perfect 15–0 season by demolishing Texas Christian University (TCU) 65–7 to win its second straight title.

FACT BOX

First Season: 1892

Location: Athens, Georgia

Stadium: Sanford Stadium

Conference: Southeastern Conference

All-Time Record: 892–432–54

Bowl Record: 38–22–3

National Titles: 1942,* 1980, 2021, 2022

College Football Playoff Appearances: 2017, 2021, 2022, 2024

Top Coaches: Wallace Butts (1939–60); Vince Dooley (1964–88); Mark Richt (2001–15); Kirby Smart (2016–)

Top Players: Frank Sinkwich (1940–42); Charley Trippi (1942, 1945–46); Herschel Walker (1980–82); Terry Hoage (1980–83); David Pollack (2001–04); Nick Chubb (2014–17); Stetson Bennett (2019–22); Brock Bowers (2021–23)

Mascot: Uga, Hairy Dawg

*Title claimed by school, though not recognized by the NCAA.

GEORGIA TECH YELLOW JACKETS

Georgia Tech was one of the first powerhouse teams in college football. The Yellow Jackets were coached by the legendary John Heisman in the early 1900s. Between 1915 and 1917, Heisman led the school to a three-year record of 24–0–2. The 1917 team was nicknamed "The Golden Tornado" and won the school's first national title.

Heisman left the team in 1919, but new coach William Alexander kept the success going. In 1928, he led the Yellow

"The Ramblin' Wreck," a 1930 Model A Ford, leads Georgia Tech onto the field.

Georgia Tech's Keith Holmes blocks a field goal against Nebraska in the Citrus Bowl on January 1, 1991.

Jackets to a 10–0 record and the school's second championship. Georgia Tech also played in its first bowl game that season. The Yellow Jackets defeated California 8–7 in the Rose Bowl.

The Yellow Jackets' longest serving coach took the helm in 1945. Bobby Dodd had only two losing seasons before leaving the program in 1967. His teams also won the Sugar Bowl three times and the Orange Bowl twice. Today, the Yellow Jackets play their games in Bobby Dodd Stadium.

Georgia Tech struggled through the 1970s and early 1980s. But coach Bobby Ross turned the team around after he was hired in 1987. Though he won only five games in his first two

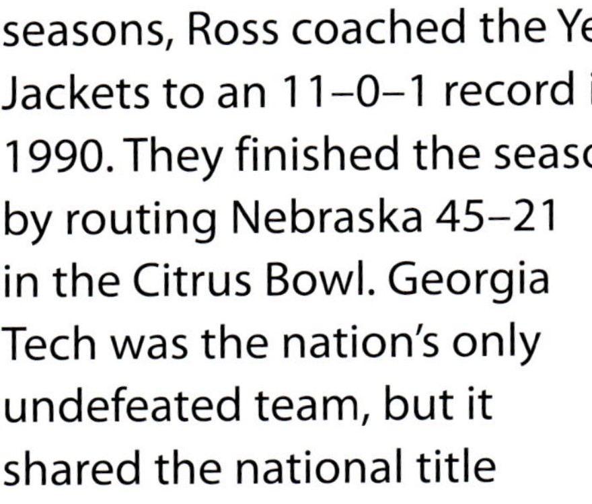

seasons, Ross coached the Yellow Jackets to an 11–0–1 record in 1990. They finished the season by routing Nebraska 45–21 in the Citrus Bowl. Georgia Tech was the nation's only undefeated team, but it shared the national title with Colorado.

Ross left the Yellow Jackets in 1992. After another brief slump, Georgia Tech began a streak of 18 straight bowl games in 1997. During that time, fans in Atlanta were thrilled by the performances of record-smashing quarterback Joe Hamilton and dominant receiver Calvin Johnson.

Wide receiver Calvin Johnson is Georgia Tech's career leader in touchdown catches with 28.

THE BIGGEST BLOWOUT

In the spring of 1915, Georgia Tech's baseball team lost 22–0 to Cumberland College. Later, Georgia Tech discovered Cumberland had illegally used professional players for the game. When Cumberland came to Atlanta to play a football game in the fall of 1916, Yellow Jackets coach John Heisman took revenge. Georgia Tech scored on 18 of its 28 offensive plays. The Yellow Jackets also scored seven defensive touchdowns and returned six kicks for scores. The 222–0 final is still the most lopsided game in college football history.

FACT BOX

First Season: 1892

Location: Atlanta, Georgia

Stadium: Bobby Dodd Stadium

Conference: Atlantic Coast Conference

All-Time Record: 763–546–43

Bowl Record: 26–21

National Titles: 1917, 1928, 1952,* *1990*

College Football Playoff Appearances: None

Top Coaches: John Heisman (1904–19); William Alexander (1920–44); Bobby Dodd (1945–66)

Top Players: Bill Fincher (1916–20); Maxie Baughan (1957–59); Randy Rhino (1972–74); Robert Lavette (1981–84); Pat Swilling (1982–85); Joe Hamilton (1996–99); Calvin Johnson (2004–06)

Mascot: Buzz, The Ramblin' Wreck

*Title claimed by school, though not recognized by the NCAA.

Shared National Titles in Italics

College football surged in popularity during the 1920s. The University of Illinois had one of the sport's biggest stars. Running back Red Grange became a national sensation while leading the team to a national title in 1923.

Running back Red Grange was an All-American three times while at Illinois.

A year later, Illinois hosted Michigan in the first game at the school's new Memorial Stadium. Grange took the opening kickoff 95 yards for a touchdown. He added four more long touchdown runs and passed for another score. Illinois beat the Wolverines 39–14.

After the game, celebrated writer Grantland Rice penned a poem. He referred to Grange as a "gray ghost." Chicago sportswriter Warren Brown then nicknamed Grange "The Galloping Ghost."

Illinois running back Robert Holcombe (35) became the team's all-time leading rusher after piling up 4,059 yards from 1994 to 1997.

Grange played for coach Robert Zuppke. The innovative coach won 131 games at Illinois between 1913 and 1941. Ray Eliot then took over and led the school to two Rose Bowls over his 18 seasons. After the 1951 season, Illinois defeated Stanford 40–7 in the Rose Bowl to cap a 9–0–1 season. The school claimed a national title after the win.

Illinois won the Rose Bowl again after the 1963 season. But the Fighting Illini didn't win the Big Ten again until 1983. That year, coach Mike White led Illinois to its first ten-win season since 1902.

The team struggled for consistency throughout the 1990s and 2000s. Between 1993 and 2006, Illinois went to only three bowl games, though one was a Sugar Bowl appearance after a ten-win season in 2001. In 2007, coach Ron Zook took Illinois back to the Rose Bowl. It was the team's first appearance in the game in 24 years. In 2024, Bret Bielema led Illinois to just its fifth ten-win season. The Fighting Illini capped the year with a 21–17 win over South Carolina in the Citrus Bowl.

Illinois quarterback Luke Altmyer throws a pass against Michigan in 2024. The Fighting Illini wore throwback uniforms for the game to celebrate the team's famous 1924 win over Michigan.

MASCOT REMOVED

Beginning in 1926, Chief Illiniwek was the mascot for the University of Illinois. In 2005, the NCAA ruled the mascot offensive to native peoples. The school officially retired Chief Illiniwek in 2007. The school has not used an official mascot since.

FACT BOX

First Season: 1890

Location: Champaign, Illinois

Stadium: Memorial Stadium

Conference: Big Ten Conference

All-Time Record: 642–628–50

Bowl Record: 9–12

National Titles: 1914,* *1919*, *1923*, *1927*, 1951*

College Football Playoff Appearances: None

Top Coaches: Robert Zuppke (1913–41); Ray Eliot (1942–59); Mike White (1980–87)

Top Players: Red Grange (1923–25); Dick Butkus (1962–64); David Williams (1983–85); Moe Gardner (1987–90); Kevin Hardy (1992–95); Kurt Kittner (1998–2001)

Mascot: None

*Title claimed by school, though not recognized by the NCAA.

Shared National Titles in Italics

IOWA HAWKEYES

Though Iowa began playing football in 1889, the school didn't make much of a national impression until 1939. That year, shifty halfback Nile Kinnick won the school's first Heisman Trophy. "The Cornbelt Comet" also helped turn around a team that had won just two games combined in the previous two seasons. Kinnick led Iowa to a 6–1–1 record in 1939. Today, the stadium in Iowa City is named after him.

Coach Forest Evashevski took the Hawkeyes to their first Rose Bowl after the 1956 season. Iowa routed Oregon State 35–19. Two years later, Evashevski's Hawkeyes went back to the Rose Bowl. After beating California 38–12, Iowa claimed a share of the national title.

Coach Hayden Fry took over a struggling team in 1979.

Iowa's Nile Kinnick threw for 638 yards and 11 touchdowns while rushing for 374 yards in 1939. He also had eight interceptions on defense.

He won the Big Ten in his third season. That kicked off a stretch of eight consecutive bowl-game appearances for the Hawkeyes.

Kirk Ferentz was an assistant to Fry during that stretch. When Fry stepped down after the 1998 season, Ferentz took over. The Hawkeyes went 10–4 in 2023. It was their eighth ten-win season under Ferentz. In the 100 years before he became coach, Iowa had just three ten-win seasons. Ferentz's Hawkeyes were also consistent. In 2024, he guided Iowa to a bowl game for the 21st time in 26 seasons.

Iowa has many long-standing rivalries in the Big Ten. One of its biggest is with neighbor Minnesota. Each season since 1935, the schools have played for a cast-iron pig named Floyd of Rosedale. In 2024, Iowa won the pig for the 45th time in 90 trophy meetings. The teams have tied twice.

Iowa quarterback Chuck Long finished second in the 1985 Heisman Trophy voting while leading the Hawkeyes to the Rose Bowl.

Iowa players hold up Floyd of Rosedale after beating Minnesota in the teams' September 2024 game. The rivals have been playing for the trophy since 1935.

THE HAWKEYE WAVE

Kinnick Stadium sits just below the University of Iowa's Stead Family Children's Hospital. Patients are able to see the game from their windows. At the end of the first quarter, fans and players from both teams turn toward the hospital and wave to the children inside. Each game, a patient is chosen as a "kid captain." The captain selects a song to play during the wave.

FACT BOX

First Season: 1889

Location: Iowa City, Iowa

Stadium: Kinnick Stadium

Conference: Big Ten Conference

All-Time Record: 701–581–39

Bowl Record: 18–18–1

National Titles: 1921,* 1922,* 1956,* *1958*, 1960*

College Football Playoff Appearances: None

Top Coaches: Forest Evashevski (1952–60); Hayden Fry (1979–98); Kirk Ferentz (1999–)

Top Players: Duke Slater (1918–21); Nile Kinnick (1937–39); Cal Jones (1953–55); Alex Karras (1956–57); Andre Tippett (1979–81); Chuck Long (1982–85); Larry Station (1982–85); Robert Gallery (2000–03)

Mascot: Herky the Hawk

*Title claimed by school, though not recognized by the NCAA.

Shared National Titles in Italics

KANSAS STATE WILDCATS

Beginning in 1989, coach Bill Snyder won 215 games at Kansas State. No coach who came before him won more than 33.

For many of its first 91 seasons, Kansas State football was a struggling program. From 1939 to 1988, the team posted a winning record only three times. Meanwhile, the Wildcats went winless seven times in that span.

The school hired coach Bill Snyder in 1989, hoping he could turn things around. After three losing records in his first four seasons, Snyder did just that. He built Kansas State into an annual bowl team. Snyder delivered the school's first bowl win in 1993. The Wildcats knocked off Wyoming 52–17 in the Copper Bowl. Three years later, Kansas State played in its first major bowl game when it appeared in the Cotton Bowl. In 1997, Snyder's team won the Fiesta Bowl 35–18 over Syracuse to cap an 11–1 season.

The Wildcats came close to a national title in 1998. After the regular season, Kansas State was 11–0 and ranked No. 1 in the BCS standings. However, it lost the Big 12 Championship

Game to Texas A&M 36–33 on a stunning touchdown pass by the Aggies in double overtime.

Snyder left the team after the 2005 season. But with the Wildcats struggling, he returned in 2009. Kansas State went to eight consecutive bowl games

Kansas State quarterback Michael Bishop fires a pass during the Fiesta Bowl on December 31, 1997.

between 2010 and 2017. Snyder retired for good in 2018. The Wildcats now play in a stadium named after Snyder.

Chris Klieman took over in 2019 and kept the Wildcats on a winning track. He took Kansas State to five bowl appearances in his first six seasons. The highlight was a Sugar Bowl appearance after the 2022 season.

Running back Darren Sproles left Kansas State in 2004 as the school's all-time rushing leader with 4,979 yards and 45 touchdowns.

THE SUNFLOWER SHOWDOWN

Kansas State forms half of one of the longest-running rivalries in college football. Each season, the Wildcats face the Kansas Jayhawks for the Governor's Cup. The teams first met in 1902 and have played every year since 1911. Only five rivalries have a longer continuous streak than the Sunflower Showdown. In 2024, the Wildcats beat the Jayhawks for the 16th year in a row.

FACT BOX

First Season: 1896

Location: Manhattan, Kansas

Stadium: Bill Snyder Family Stadium

Conference: Big 12 Conference

All-Time Record: 579–674–42

Bowl Record: 12–14

National Titles: None

College Football Playoff Appearances: None

Top Coaches: Bill Snyder (1989–2005, 2009–18); Chris Klieman (2019–)

Top Players: Lynn Dickey (1968–70); Steve Grogan (1972–74); Mark Simoneau (1996–99); Michael Bishop (1997–98); Darren Sproles (2001–04); Collin Klein (2009–12); Tyler Lockett (2011–14)

Mascot: Willie the Wildcat

LOUISVILLE CARDINALS

Louisville wide receiver Mark Clayton makes a move against Pittsburgh during a game in October 1982.

Louisville played as an independent program from its founding in 1912 through the 1962 season. In that time, the Cardinals reached only one bowl game. The school's biggest claim to fame was quarterback Johnny Unitas. He played at Louisville from 1951 to 1954 before starting a legendary NFL career. After a brief stint in the Missouri Valley Conference, Louisville became independent again in 1975.

The Cardinals didn't achieve national success until Louisville native Howard Schnellenberger took over as coach in the 1980s. Schnellenberger had earlier led the Miami Hurricanes to a national title. The Cardinals were coming off a 2–9 season when he arrived in 1985. By 1990, they were a top-25 team.

Louisville finished 10–1–1 that year. That included a 34–7 rout over Alabama in the Fiesta Bowl.

Schnellenberger left the program after the 1994 season. The team initially struggled. But coach John L. Smith turned things around in the late 1990s. Over a 27-year span from 1998 to 2024, the Cardinals played in a bowl game 22 times. They also bounced between conferences before joining the powerhouse ACC in 2014.

Louisville's Sheldon Rankins takes down Florida quarterback Jeff Driskel in the Sugar Bowl on January 2, 2013. Louisville won the game 33–23.

Louisville developed a strong line of quarterbacks. Chris Redman set the school's record by throwing for 12,541 yards and 84 touchdowns between 1996 and 1999. In the 2000s, both Brian Brohm and Teddy Bridgewater threw for more than 9,000 yards before they were drafted by NFL teams. Brohm led the Cardinals to an Orange Bowl victory in January 2007. Bridgewater beat Florida in the Sugar Bowl after the 2012 season.

In 2016, electrifying dual-threat quarterback Lamar Jackson became Louisville's first Heisman Trophy winner. That year, Jackson threw for 3,543 yards and 30 touchdowns. He added another 21 touchdowns on the ground.

MEET THE BROHMS

The Brohm family has a long history with Louisville football. Oscar Brohm was the school's quarterback in the late 1960s. His sons Jeff and Greg played for Howard Schnellenberger in the late 1980s and early 1990s. His youngest son, Brian, quarterbacked Louisville from 2004 to 2007. Jeff was hired as the school's head coach in December 2022. He hired both of his brothers as assistants.

FACT BOX

First Season: 1912

Location: Louisville, Kentucky

Stadium: L&N Federal Credit Union Stadium

Conference: Atlantic Coast Conference

All-Time Record: 559–500–17

Bowl Record: 13–13–1

National Titles: None

College Football Playoff Appearances: None

Top Coaches: John L. Smith (1998–2002); Bobby Petrino (2003–06, 2014–18); Charlie Strong (2010–13)

Top Players: Johnny Unitas (1951–54); Tom Jackson (1970–72); Otis Wilson (1977–79); Roman Oben (1992–95); Chris Redman (1996–99); Teddy Bridgewater (2011–13); Lamar Jackson (2015–17)

Mascot: Louie the Cardinal

Cardinals quarterback Lamar Jackson was just 19 years, 337 days old when he won the 2016 Heisman Trophy. That made him the youngest player ever to win the award.

LSU TIGERS

Louisiana State University's (LSU's) Tiger Stadium has long been an intimidating place to play. The huge stadium is nicknamed "Death Valley." Noise levels can reach 130 decibels, which is as loud as a jet taking off. The school's mascot, a live tiger named Mike, is on the sideline. Most LSU home games are played at night. That way, the teams can avoid the legendary Louisiana heat. But playing under the lights also adds excitement.

LSU running back Billy Cannon became the team's first Heisman Trophy winner when he took home the award in 1959.

LSU running back Justin Vincent (25) scores a touchdown against Oklahoma in the Sugar Bowl on January 4, 2004.

The Tigers have a history of dominant teams. In 1958, star running back Billy Cannon led LSU to an 11–0 record. The Tigers allowed more than 10 points in only one game. After the season, both major polls named LSU the national champion.

Some great players came through Baton Rouge after that, including defensive back Tommy Casanova and running back Kevin Faulk. However, the Tigers didn't get back to No. 1 in the 1900s. In 2003, coach Nick Saban led LSU to the BCS Championship Game. The Tigers knocked off Oklahoma 21–14. Defensive tackle Marcus Spears provided the key play. He returned an interception 20 yards for a touchdown in the third

UNIQUE FEATURES

Tiger Stadium still features old-fashioned goalposts, which are shaped like an H. That way, LSU's players can run through them when they enter the field. Also, while most fields feature painted numbers every 10 yards, Tiger Stadium has a number painted every five yards.

quarter for what proved to be the winning score.

Four years later, coach Les Miles's Tigers lost a pair of triple-overtime games during the regular season. But LSU still reached the national title game. The Tigers routed Ohio State 38–24 to become the first national champion with two losses since 1960.

Tigers quarterback Joe Burrow won the 2019 Heisman Trophy by a record-setting margin.

LSU's next championship came after the 2019 season. Coach Ed Orgeron had perhaps the most talented team in school history. Heisman Trophy–winning quarterback Joe Burrow set an FBS record with 60 touchdown passes. It helped having future NFL stars Ja'Marr Chase and Justin Jefferson as receivers. The Tigers averaged nearly 50 points per game. LSU extended its dominance into the College Football Playoff. The Tigers smothered Oklahoma 63–28 in the semifinals behind seven touchdown passes from Burrow. LSU then pulled away from defending champion Clemson in the second half of the title game. Burrow threw five more touchdowns in a 42–25 win.

FACT BOX

First Season: 1893

Location: Baton Rouge, Louisiana

Stadium: Tiger Stadium

Conference: Southeastern Conference

All-Time Record: 815–438–47

Bowl Record: 31–24–1

National Titles: *1958*, *2003*, 2007, 2019

College Football Playoff Appearances: 2019

Top Coaches: Charles McClendon (1962–79); Les Miles (2005–16); Ed Orgeron (2016–21)

Top Players: Billy Cannon (1957–59); Tommy Casanova (1969–71); Kevin Faulk (1995–98); Glenn Dorsey (2004–07); Joe Burrow (2018–19); Derek Stingley Jr. (2019–21); Malik Nabers (2021–23); Jayden Daniels (2022–23)

Mascot: Mike the Tiger

Shared National Titles in Italics

MIAMI HURRICANES

Miami didn't have much football history until coach Howard Schnellenberger was hired in 1979. He quickly built up the program by recruiting heavily in the talent-rich state of Florida. That process paid off when the Hurricanes won their first national championship after the 1983 season.

Even though Schnellenberger left after that, Miami's win kicked off a dominant decade of college football for the school known as "The U." Miami was ranked No. 1 in the Associated

Coach Howard Schnellenberger went 41–16 during his five seasons at Miami from 1979 to 1983.

Miami receiver Kevin Williams makes a touchdown catch in the Orange Bowl against Nebraska on January 1, 1992. The win secured the Hurricanes' fourth national championship.

Press poll at some point in every season but one from 1983 through 1992. The Hurricanes were a fearsome team and often hated by opponents. Miami's rivals accused the flashy Hurricanes of poor sportsmanship.

Schnellenberger's replacement, Jimmy Johnson, never tried to stop his players' swagger. In 1987, the Hurricanes strutted their way to an 11–0 regular season. They faced the also undefeated Oklahoma Sooners in the Orange Bowl. Miami held on for a 20–14 victory to clinch the national championship.

Johnson won another title in 1989 before moving on to the NFL. New coach Dennis Erickson stepped in and kept Miami on top. The 1991 Hurricanes went into the Orange Bowl ranked

Miami running back Clinton Portis breaks away for a 39-yard touchdown run in the Orange Bowl on January 3, 2002.

No. 1 with an 11–0 record. They then shut out Nebraska to clinch a fourth championship.

Miami's success came crashing down in the mid-1990s when a series of scandals landed the football team on probation. The infractions were so bad that *Sports Illustrated* magazine famously suggested the school stop fielding a team. But Miami bounced back in the early 2000s. Coach Larry Coker led a star-studded 11–0 team into the Rose Bowl after the 2001 season. Miami closed out its fifth title by routing Nebraska again. This time the Hurricanes won 37–14.

THE BEST TEAM EVER?

Miami's 2001 national-championship roster was filled with NFL talent. The team had 11 players taken in the 2002 draft, including five first-round picks. By the time all the players had left Miami, 38 of them had been drafted by NFL teams. Seventeen of those players were taken in the first round.

FACT BOX

First Season: 1926

Location: Coral Gables, Florida

Stadium: Hard Rock Stadium

Conference: Atlantic Coast Conference

All-Time Record: 673–391–19

Bowl Record: 20–24

National Titles: 1983, 1987, 1989, *1991*, 2001

College Football Playoff Appearances: None

Top Coaches: Howard Schnellenberger (1979–83); Jimmy Johnson (1984–88); Larry Coker (2001–06)

Top Players: Ted Hendricks (1966–68); Vinny Testaverde (1982–86); Bennie Blades (1985–87); Gino Torretta (1989–92); Warren Sapp (1992–94); Ray Lewis (1993–95); Ed Reed (1998–2001); Willis McGahee (2001–02)

Mascot: Sebastian the Ibis

Shared National Titles in Italics

MICHIGAN WOLVERINES

Michigan won its first game on May 30, 1879. On November 18, 2023, the Wolverines won for the 1,000th time. With the 31–24 victory over Maryland, Michigan became the first FBS school to reach that milestone.

Many of the school's record wins have been memorable. In January 1902, Michigan routed Stanford 49–0 in the first Rose Bowl. No Big Ten team has appeared in the storied game more times than the Wolverines. However, the wins that Michigan fans look forward to the most are those that come against neighbor and fierce rival Ohio State. Their annual end-of-season matchup is known simply as "The Game."

Michigan Stadium, also known as "The Big House," is the largest stadium in the country.

Few rivalries in all of sports compare to Michigan and Ohio State. The bitterness between the two teams peaked between 1969 and 1978. The Wolverines, led by legendary coach Bo Schembechler, squared off with Woody Hayes's Buckeyes in what became known as "The Ten Year War."

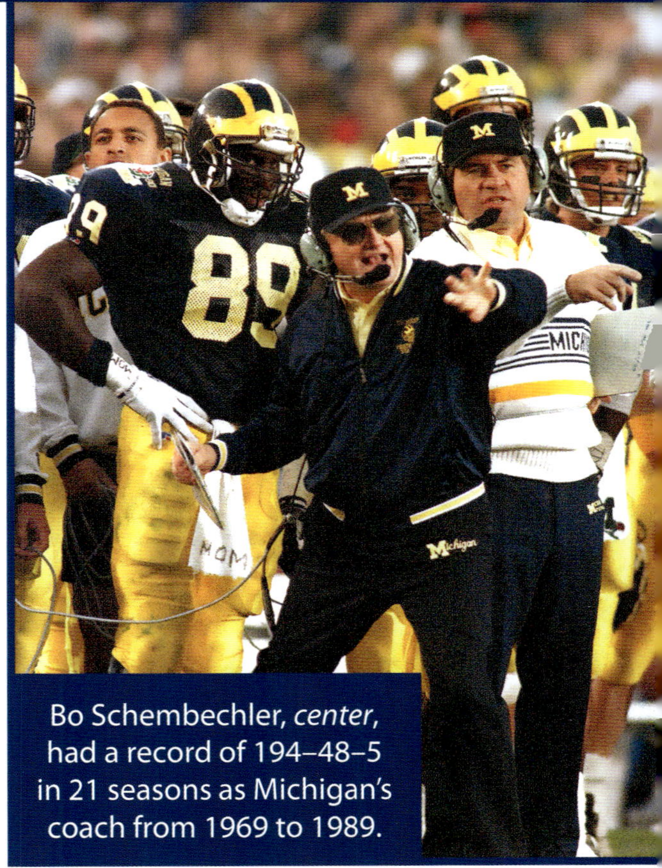

Bo Schembechler, *center*, had a record of 194–48–5 in 21 seasons as Michigan's coach from 1969 to 1989.

Michigan boasts many legends and traditions. The team's "winged" helmet design is iconic. Its home stadium is nicknamed "The Big House." Holding more than 107,000 fans, it's the biggest in college football. The Wolverines also enjoy long-standing rivalries with Illinois, Michigan State, and Minnesota, though another one with Notre Dame has been paused.

Three Wolverines have won the Heisman Trophy. The first was running back Tom Harmon in 1940. Harmon's career was legendary enough that no player wore his No. 98 jersey for another 73 years. Electrifying receiver Desmond Howard won the award in 1991. And in 1997, cornerback Charles Woodson made history when he became the first defensive player to win the Heisman.

Despite Michigan's success, the team went into the 2023 season seeking its first outright national title since 1948. Behind legendary player-turned-coach Jim Harbaugh, the team rode the nation's best defense to a 13–0 record. In the College Football Playoff, Michigan rallied to beat Alabama 27–20 in overtime in the semifinal round. The Wolverines then thumped Washington 34–13 in the championship game to capture the program's 12th national crown.

Running back Blake Corum bursts through a hole for one of his two touchdowns in Michigan's National Championship Game win on January 8, 2024.

STOPPING IN SOUTH BEND

Michigan was on its way to play a game in Chicago in 1887 when the players stopped in South Bend, Indiana. While there, the Wolverines introduced football to the University of Notre Dame. The demonstration helped create the storied Notre Dame program. The two schools eventually became bitter rivals.

FACT BOX

First Season: 1879

Location: Ann Arbor, Michigan

Stadium: Michigan Stadium

Conference: Big Ten Conference

All-Time Record: 1,012–358–36

Bowl Record: 24–29

National Titles: 1901, 1902, *1903*, *1904*, *1918*, *1923*, 1932,* 1933, 1947,* 1948, *1997*, 2023

College Football Playoff Appearances: 2021, 2022, 2023

Top Coaches: Fielding Yost (1901–23, 1925–26); Bo Schembechler (1969–89); Lloyd Carr (1995–2007); Jim Harbaugh (2015–23)

Top Players: Bennie Oosterbaan (1925–27); Tom Harmon (1938–40); Anthony Carter (1979–82); Jim Harbaugh (1983–86); Desmond Howard (1989–91); Charles Woodson (1995–97); Aidan Hutchinson (2018–21)

*Title claimed by school, though not recognized by the NCAA.

Shared National Titles in Italics

MICHIGAN STATE SPARTANS

Michigan State's football history is often overshadowed. The Spartans compete in a region filled with historic teams such as Michigan, Ohio State, and Notre Dame. But the Spartans have their own long, rich tradition of winning football.

Michigan State operated as an independent team from 1896 to 1952. Coach Biggie Munn led the Spartans to back-to-back 9–0 seasons in 1951 and 1952. The next year, Michigan State joined the Big Ten. The Spartans won both the conference and the Rose Bowl in two of their first three Big Ten seasons.

The second of those Rose Bowl wins came under second-year coach Hugh "Duffy" Daugherty. The school's all-time winningest coach led the Spartans from 1954 to 1972. He built another powerhouse team in the mid-1960s. The Spartans won their

Coach Hugh "Duffy" Daugherty had a record of 109–69–5 in 19 seasons at Michigan State from 1954 to 1972.

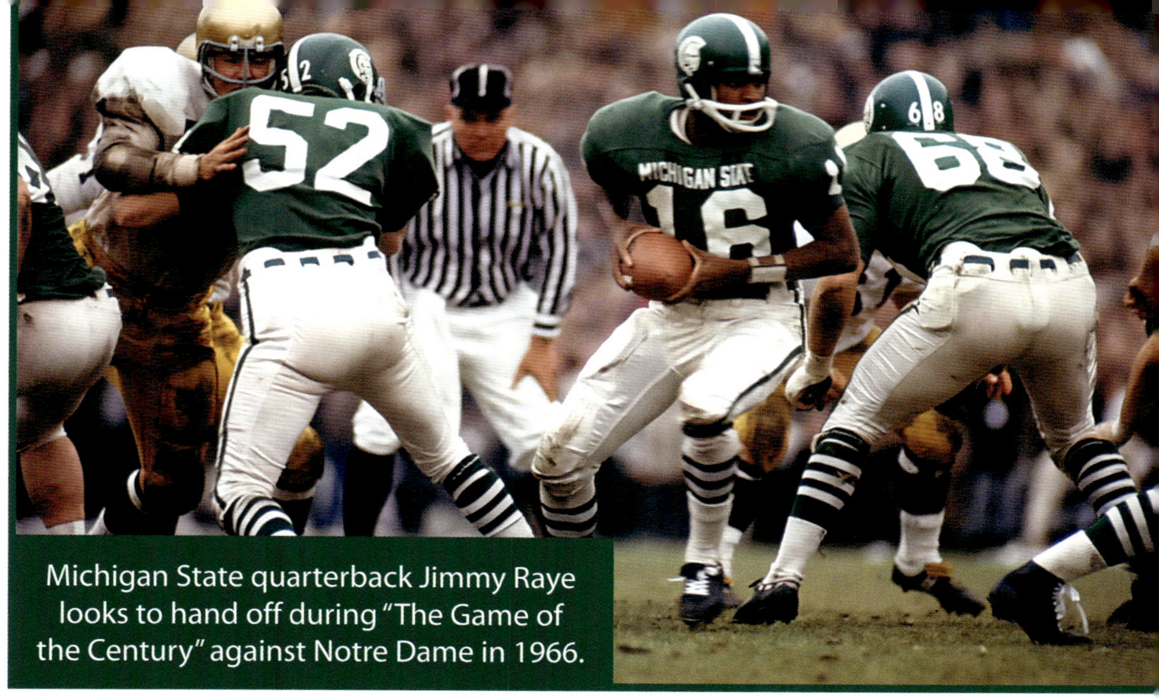

Michigan State quarterback Jimmy Raye looks to hand off during "The Game of the Century" against Notre Dame in 1966.

fifth national title in 1965. That year's team boasted the strong running of Clinton Jones and a defense that allowed fewer than six points per game.

The following year, Michigan State hosted Notre Dame in a late-season contest dubbed "The Game of the Century." The Spartans came into the game with a 9–0 record and a

PENNIES FOR LUCK

Before every home game, the Michigan State players make their "Spartan Walk" from the Kellogg Hotel to Spartan Stadium. On the way, they pass the Spartan Statue. The players traditionally toss pennies at the giant bronze statue's feet for good luck.

No. 2 ranking. The top-ranked Fighting Irish were 8–0. In a hard-fought battle, the teams were tied 10–10 late in the game. Notre Dame coach Ara Parseghian elected to run out the clock rather than go for a winning score. After the controversial tie, both schools claimed to be national champions.

Michigan State has played in only two Rose Bowls since its appearance after the 1965 season. The first came in 1987 under coach George Perles. Mark Dantonio took Michigan State back to the game in Pasadena, California, after the 2013 season.

FACT BOX

First Season: 1896

Location: East Lansing, Michigan

Stadium: Spartan Stadium

Conference: Big Ten Conference

All-Time Record: 735–494–44

Bowl Record: 14–16

National Titles: 1951,* 1952, 1955,* 1957,* *1965*, *1966*

College Football Playoff Appearances: 2015

Top Coaches: Clarence "Biggie" Munn (1947–53); Duffy Daugherty (1954–72); Mark Dantonio (2007–19)

Top Players: Don Coleman (1949–51); Clinton Jones (1964–66); Bubba Smith (1964–66); George Webster (1964–66); Lorenzo White (1984–87); Percy Snow (1986–89); Charles Rogers (2001–02); Connor Cook (2012–15)

Mascot: Sparty

*Title claimed by school, though not recognized by the NCAA.

Shared National Titles in Italics

Michigan State's mascot, Sparty, plants the school flag at the Rose Bowl in January 2014. Michigan State beat Stanford 24–20 to complete the school's first 13-win season.

MINNESOTA GOLDEN GOPHERS

Minnesota was one of the founding members of the Western Conference in the 1890s. Today, that conference is known as the Big Ten. The Golden Gophers were also one of the conference's first powers.

The Gophers reached their greatest heights in the 1930s under Bernie Bierman. The legendary coach didn't lose a game between 1933 and 1935. The Gophers claimed national titles after finishing 8–0 in both 1934 and 1935. Minnesota won the national title for a third straight season in 1936 with a 7–1 mark.

Bierman led the Gophers to another pair of 8–0 seasons in 1940 and 1941. His star player was speedy,

Minnesota running back Bruce Smith poses with the Heisman Trophy after winning the award in 1941.

Minnesota's Sandy Stephens (15) runs with the ball against Illinois in 1961. That season, Stephens became the first Black quarterback to earn First-Team All-America honors.

versatile running back Bruce Smith. The team won national titles in both years. In 1941, Smith became the school's first Heisman Trophy winner.

Coach Murray Warmath took over in 1954. In 1960, he guided the Gophers to their first Rose Bowl, but they lost 17–7 to Washington. At the time, national champions were named before bowl games were played. The Gophers had already been crowned title winners before the game was played. A year later, Minnesota won its first Rose Bowl by beating UCLA 21–3.

For almost 40 seasons, the Gophers reached only three bowl games. But coach Glen Mason began a turnaround. Building around great running backs, his Minnesota teams reached bowl games in seven of eight seasons from 1999 to 2006. In January 2025, coach P. J. Fleck led the Gophers to victory in the Duke's Mayo Bowl. It was Minnesota's eighth consecutive bowl victory.

Minnesota wide receiver Tyler Johnson celebrates with Paul Bunyan's Axe after the Gophers won the rivalry trophy from Wisconsin in 2018.

OLD RIVALRIES

Minnesota and Michigan have competed for the Little Brown Jug since 1909. Minnesota and Iowa began battling for Floyd of Rosedale in 1935. But Minnesota's oldest rivalry is with neighboring Wisconsin. The teams first met in 1890 and have played every year since 1907. That makes it the longest continuous rivalry in college football's top level. The winner claims Paul Bunyan's Axe.

FACT BOX

First Season: 1882

Location: Minneapolis, Minnesota

Stadium: Huntington Bank Stadium

Conference: Big Ten Conference

All-Time Record: 741–548–44

Bowl Record: 13–12

National Titles: 1904,* 1934, 1935, 1936, 1940, 1941, *1960*

College Football Playoff Appearances: None

Top Coaches: Henry Williams (1900–21); Bernie Bierman (1932–41, 1945–50); Murray Warmath (1954–71)

Top Players: Bronko Nagurski (1927–29); Bruce Smith (1939–41); Paul Giel (1951–53); Sandy Stephens (1959–61); Bobby Bell (1960–62); Darrell Thompson (1986–89); Tyler Johnson (2016–19); Mohamed Ibrahim (2018–22)

Mascot: Goldy Gopher

*Title claimed by school, though not recognized by the NCAA.

Shared National Titles in Italics

NEBRASKA CORNHUSKERS

Nebraska began a sellout streak at Memorial Stadium in 1962. It was still going in 2025 at more than 400 consecutive sellouts.

Nebraska built a strong football tradition on a powerful option-based run game and fierce defense. Starting in the 1960s, coach Bob Devaney turned the Cornhuskers into a national power. Devaney's team won its first major bowl game by beating Auburn 13–7 in the Orange Bowl after the 1963 season.

In 1970, Devaney led the Cornhuskers to their first national title. The Huskers were on their way to another dominant season the next year when they traveled to Oklahoma to face their rival on Thanksgiving Day. Nebraska's star wide receiver Johnny Rodgers weaved 72 yards for a touchdown on an early punt return. The play is considered one of the most exciting in college football history. Nebraska won the game 35–31 on its way to a second title. A year later, Rodgers became the school's first Heisman Trophy winner.

Tom Osborne took over for Devaney in 1973. Osborne put together national title contenders nearly every season. But he had to wait a long time to claim the ultimate prize.

Cornhuskers wide receiver Johnny Rodgers (20) runs away from two Alabama defenders in the Orange Bowl on January 1, 1972.

After several heartbreaking losses in the 1980s, Osborne's Cornhuskers broke through in 1994. The team held off Miami 24–17 in the Orange Bowl to cap a perfect 13–0 season. The following season, Nebraska routed Florida 62–24 in the Fiesta Bowl. The highlight of the game was

THE BLACKSHIRTS

In 1964, Nebraska coach Bob Devaney gave his defense black jerseys to wear in practice. Soon, the defense was labeled "The Blackshirts." Eventually, earning a black practice shirt became an honor for a Nebraska defender.

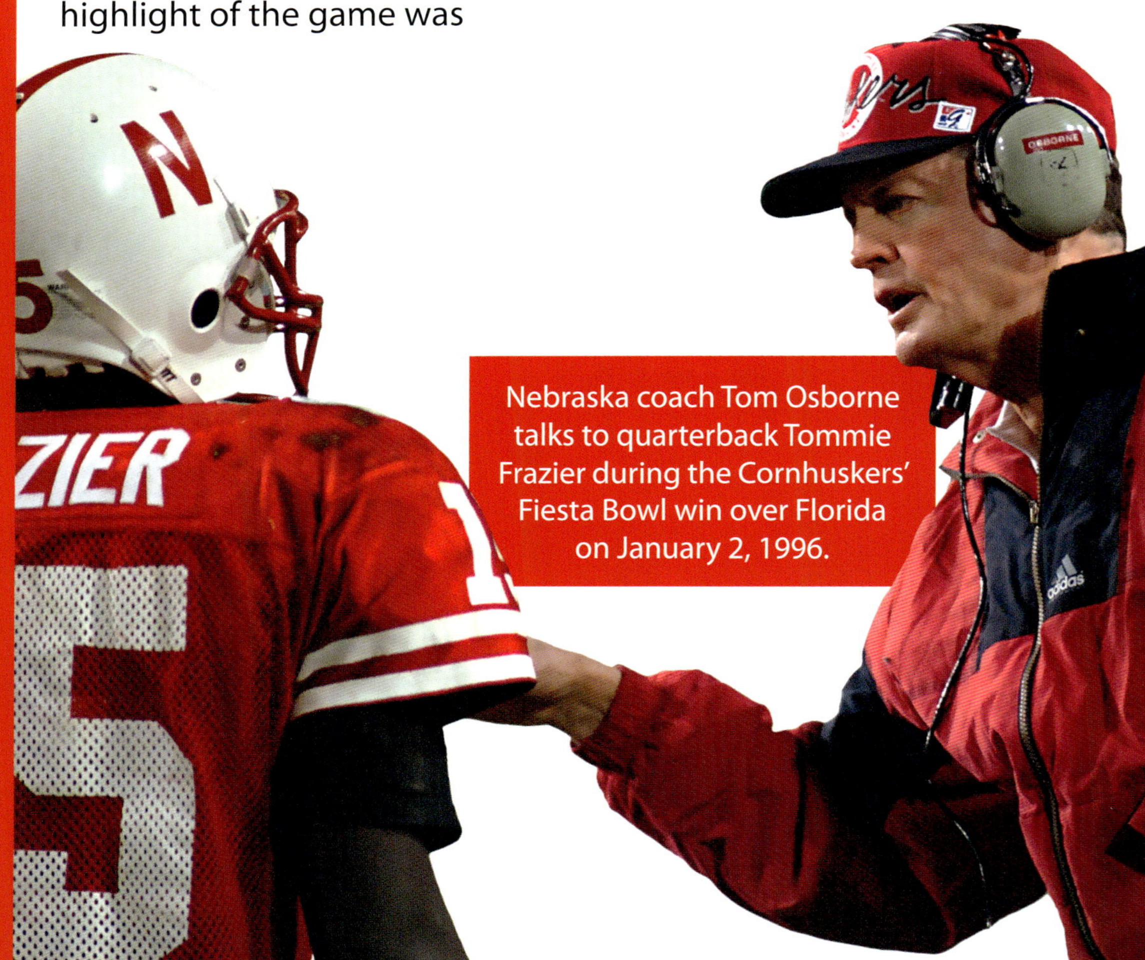

Nebraska coach Tom Osborne talks to quarterback Tommie Frazier during the Cornhuskers' Fiesta Bowl win over Florida on January 2, 1996.

a 75-yard run from quarterback Tommie Frazier in the fourth quarter. Several Florida defenders appeared to stop Frazier for a short gain before the quarterback broke free for the score.

Nebraska added one more national title in Osborne's final season in 1997. In the years since, the Cornhuskers have struggled to measure up to their history. The 2004 team finished 5–6. It was Nebraska's first losing season since 1961. The team later went seven years without going to a bowl game before returning in 2024.

FACT BOX

First Season: 1890

Location: Lincoln, Nebraska

Stadium: Memorial Stadium

Conference: Big Ten Conference

All-Time Record: 924–430–40

Bowl Record: 27–27

National Titles: *1970*, 1971, 1994, 1995, *1997*

College Football Playoff Appearances: None

Top Coaches: Bob Devaney (1962–72); Tom Osborne (1973–97); Frank Solich (1998–2003)

Top Players: Johnny Rodgers (1970–72); Dave Rimington (1979–82); Mike Rozier (1981–83); Trev Alberts (1990–93); Tommie Frazier (1992–95); Aaron Taylor (1994–97); Eric Crouch (1998–2001); Ndamukong Suh (2005–09)

Mascot: Herbie Husker, Lil' Red

Shared National Titles in Italics

Notre Dame has built a mythical reputation throughout more than a century of football success. Despite being located in a small city in northwest Indiana, the private Catholic school has a national following. Notre Dame is particularly popular with Catholic fans all over the country.

The lore of the Fighting Irish was first established in the 1920s under legendary coach Knute Rockne. In 1924, "The Four Horsemen" backfield of Jim Crowley, Don Miller, Elmer Layden, and Harry Stuhldreher guided the team to its first national title. Notre Dame won its first bowl game that season by knocking off Stanford 27–10 in the Rose Bowl.

Powered by "The Four Horsemen," Notre Dame's 1924 team finished 10–0.

The Fighting Irish declined invitations to play in another bowl game for 45 years. But in an era when national champions were picked prior to the bowls being played, Notre Dame racked up several titles. The Irish were particularly successful in the 1940s, winning four national championships. The school also boasted three Heisman Trophy winners during the decade.

Notre Dame's famous "Golden Dome" helmets contain flecks of real gold.

Notre Dame's next two national championships came under coach Ara Parseghian, in 1966 and 1973. The Dan Devine–led Irish captured another title in 1977. Then Lou Holtz delivered the school's eleventh championship after the 1988 season. That year, Notre Dame went 12–0 for the first time. The team was led by dual-threat quarterback Tony Rice in 1988. A year earlier, big-play receiver Tim Brown had become Notre Dame's seventh Heisman Trophy winner.

Notre Dame has remained competitive in the years since. In 2024, coach Marcus Freeman led the Irish to the national title game before they lost to Ohio State. Even without another national title, the program continues to be uniquely popular. Every Fighting Irish game is televised nationally. And fans still flock from around the globe to take in games at historic Notre Dame Stadium.

Wide receiver Tim Brown caught 137 passes and ran the ball 98 times during his four years at Notre Dame from 1984 to 1987. He also returned kicks and punts.

TOUCHDOWN JESUS

The "Word of Life" mural overlooks Notre Dame Stadium from nearby Hesburgh Library. Completed in 1964, the mural stands 132 feet (40 m) tall and is visible from the stadium seats. The top portion of the mural depicts Jesus Christ with his arms outstretched, pointing slightly up. Since Jesus's posture resembles an official signaling a score, the mural has become known as "Touchdown Jesus."

FACT BOX

First Season: 1887

Location: Notre Dame, Indiana

Stadium: Notre Dame Stadium

Conference: Independent

All-Time Record: 962–339–42

Bowl Record: 23–22

National Titles: 1924, 1929, *1930*, 1943, 1946, 1947, 1949, *1966*, 1973, 1977, 1988

College Football Playoff Appearances: 2018, 2020, 2024

Top Coaches: Knute Rockne (1918–30); Frank Leahy (1941–43, 1946–53); Ara Parseghian (1964–74); Lou Holtz (1986–96)

Top Players: Don Miller (1922–24); Angelo Bertelli (1941–43); Johnny Lujack (1943, 1946–47); Leon Hart (1946–49); Johnny Lattner (1951–53); Paul Hornung (1954–56); John Huarte (1962–64); Tim Brown (1984–87); Manti Te'o (2009–12)

Mascot: Leprechaun

Shared National Titles in Italics

THE ARMY-NAVY GAME

Historic Rivalry

Football games between the US service academies date back to 1890, when the Black Knights of Army and Midshipmen of Navy first met. The teams have played every season since 1930. The game is usually held on the final day of the regular season. In 2024, Navy won 31–13 for its 63rd win in series history. Army had won the matchup 55 times. Both teams have strong traditions on the field. Army claims three national titles, while Navy claims one. They've combined to produce five Heisman Trophy winners.

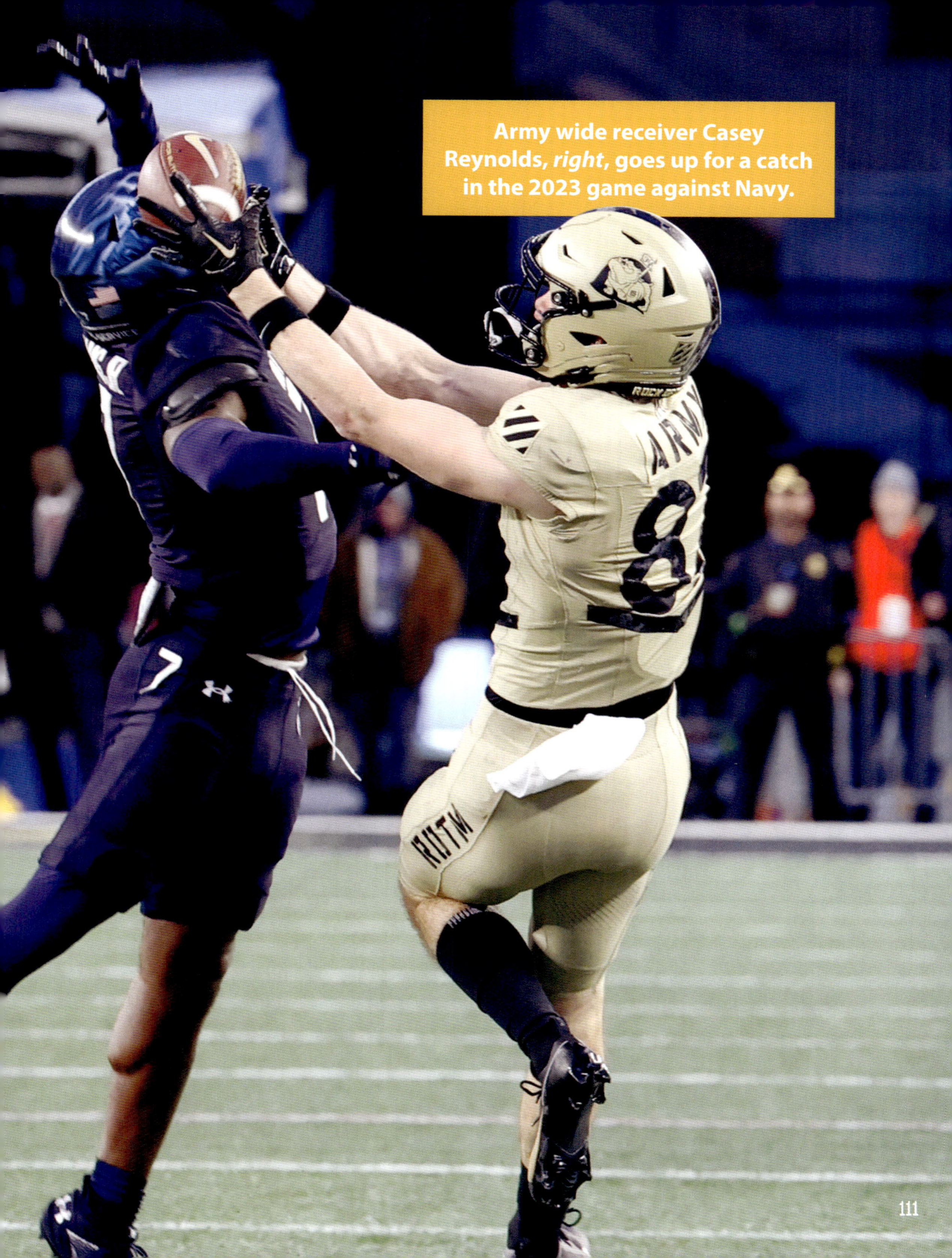

Army wide receiver Casey Reynolds, *right*, goes up for a catch in the 2023 game against Navy.

OHIO STATE BUCKEYES

Woody Hayes talks strategy with quarterback Rex Kern, *left*, in a 1968 game against Michigan.

Ohio State won its first national title in 1942 under head coach Paul Brown. Brown soon left and eventually became a legendary professional coach in Cleveland. But Ohio State hired another icon in 1951. Fiery coach Woody Hayes led the Buckeyes until 1978. His teams added five more national championships.

Hayes's best stretch came between 1968 and 1975. He took the Buckeyes to six Rose Bowls in eight seasons. During that time, he coached star running back Archie Griffin. The speedy Griffin became the first player to win the Heisman Trophy in back-to-back seasons.

Hayes may have coached Ohio State longer if it weren't for his legendary temper. During the Gator Bowl in 1978, Hayes punched a Clemson player. He resigned soon after.

All Ohio State coaches since have been measured against Hayes's record of both winning national titles and defeating archrival Michigan. Coaches who have not accomplished both have not lasted long with passionate Buckeye fans. Jim Tressel finally brought Ohio State back to the top in 2002. Led by freshman running back sensation Maurice Clarett, the Buckeyes outlasted Miami 31–24 in overtime in the Fiesta Bowl for the national title.

A dozen years later, head coach Urban Meyer took Ohio State to the first

Buckeyes running back Ezekiel Elliott scores one of his four touchdowns in the College Football Playoff National Championship Game against Oregon in January 2015.

College Football Playoff. This time, Ezekiel Elliott led the charge to the title. The bruising running back rushed for 476 total yards and six touchdowns in wins over Alabama and Oregon.

Coach Ryan Day's reputation was on the line after losing to Michigan in the finale of the 2024 season. But Day's Buckeyes regrouped for the new 12-team playoff. The team needed to win four games for the title. It did so by beating Tennessee, Oregon, Texas, and Notre Dame all by double-digit margins.

Ohio State's players celebrate after beating Notre Dame 34–23 in the National Championship Game in January 2025.

DOTTING THE "i"

Since 1937, the Ohio State marching band has performed a special routine during games. The band spells out "Ohio" in script writing. The spelling is completed by a sousaphone player who walks out and makes the dot in the "i." The sousaphone player then bows grandly to the crowd to signal the end of the performance.

FACT BOX

First Season: 1890

Location: Columbus, Ohio

Stadium: Ohio Stadium

Conference: Big Ten Conference

All-Time Record: 978–335–53

Bowl Record: 29–29

National Titles: 1942, *1954*, *1957*, *1961*, 1968, *1970*, 2002, 2014, 2024

College Football Playoff Appearances: 2014, 2016, 2019, 2020, 2022, 2024

Top Coaches: Woody Hayes (1951–78); Jim Tressel (2001–10); Urban Meyer (2012–18)

Top Players: Les Horvath (1940–42, 1944); Bill Willis (1942–44); Vic Janowicz (1949–51); Howard Cassady (1952–55); Archie Griffin (1972–75); Eddie George (1992–95); Troy Smith (2003–06); Ezekiel Elliott (2013–15)

Mascot: Brutus Buckeye

Shared National Titles in Italics

OKLAHOMA SOONERS

Much of Oklahoma's football tradition began when coach Bud Wilkinson was hired in 1947. Wilkinson put together a 31-game winning streak between 1948 and 1950. Starting in 1953, his teams won 47 straight games. Nearly 70 years later, that remained a record among FBS teams. Wilkinson coached the Sooners to three national titles before stepping down following the 1963 season.

Oklahoma coach Bud Wilkinson (in white) talks to his players before the Orange Bowl in December 1958.

Running back Steve Owens, *center*, set an Oklahoma record with 50 rushing touchdowns between 1967 and 1969. Owens won the Heisman Trophy as a senior.

Oklahoma's next great coach arrived in 1973. Using a run-focused offense, Barry Switzer led the Sooners to double-digit victories in seven of his first eight seasons. Oklahoma won the national title in 1974 and again in 1975. Switzer added a third championship in 1985. He left the team after the 1988 season without ever having a losing season.

The program was struggling in the late 1990s. That changed when Bob Stoops was hired in 1999. In his second season, Stoops and quarterback Josh Heupel led the Sooners to a 12–0 record and a spot in the Orange Bowl. Oklahoma's defense stood tall, shutting down Florida State for a 13–2 victory and a national championship.

BEDLAM

Starting in 1904, Oklahoma's annual rivalry game with Oklahoma State was always one of the highlights of each team's season. The game was known as "Bedlam" for its raucous crowds. Oklahoma dominated the game, however, winning 91 of 118 meetings. After Oklahoma moved to the SEC in 2024, Oklahoma State coach Mike Gundy declared the rivalry over.

Oklahoma's Quentin Griffin races in for the only touchdown of the Orange Bowl on January 3, 2001.

Before 2000, three Oklahoma players had won the Heisman Trophy. All three were running backs. After Stoops installed a passing offense in the 2000s, four quarterbacks won the award. Jason White was the first in 2003. Sam Bradford threw 50 touchdown passes on his way to the award in 2008. Stoops stepped down after the 2016 season. But new coach Lincoln Riley fielded Heisman-winning quarterbacks in each of his first two seasons. Baker Mayfield won the honor in 2017, and Kyler Murray won the school's seventh Heisman in 2018.

FACT BOX

First Season: 1895

Location: Norman, Oklahoma

Stadium: Gaylord Family Oklahoma Memorial Stadium

Conference: Southeastern Conference

All-Time Record: 950–348–53

Bowl Record: 31–26–1

National Titles: 1950, 1955, 1956, *1974*, 1975, 1985, 2000

College Football Playoff Appearances: 2015, 2017, 2018, 2019

Top Coaches: Bud Wilkinson (1947–63); Barry Switzer (1973–88); Bob Stoops (1991–2016, 2021)

Top Players: Billy Vessels (1950–52); Steve Owens (1967–69); Billy Sims (1975–79); Rocky Calmus (1998–2001); Jason White (1999–2004); Sam Bradford (2007–09); Baker Mayfield (2015–17); Kyler Murray (2017–18)

Mascot: Sooner Schooner

Shared National Titles in Italics

OKLAHOMA STATE COWBOYS

The school originally known as Oklahoma A&M enjoyed football success for much of the first half of the 1900s. In the 1944 season, coach Jim Lookabaugh led the Cowboys to their first bowl game. They routed TCU 34–0 in the Cotton Bowl to finish 8–1. A year later, Oklahoma A&M completed a perfect 9–0 year with a 33–13 win over Saint Mary's in the Sugar Bowl. The Cowboys claimed their only national championship that season.

The school changed its name to Oklahoma State in 1957. The football team joined the Big 8 Conference three years later. But the Cowboys struggled to keep up with powerful rivals Nebraska and Oklahoma. In the 1980s, a pair of talented running backs helped Oklahoma State improve. Thurman Thomas set a school record with 4,595 rushing yards between 1984 and 1987. He also helped the Cowboys win 34 games. After Thomas left, Barry Sanders became the starting back. The shifty

Oklahoma State mascot Pistol Pete waves to the crowd during a 2021 game at Boone Pickens Stadium.

Running back Barry Sanders breaks away for a touchdown during the Cowboys' 1988 matchup against rival Oklahoma.

runner smashed the NCAA's single-season rushing record with 2,628 rushing yards in 1988. It was one of 34 national records Sanders set as he cruised to the school's first Heisman Trophy.

Former Oklahoma State quarterback Mike Gundy took over as the team's coach in 2005. Building off the strong foundation set by former coach Les Miles, Gundy put together some of the Cowboys' finest seasons. The passionate coach led Oklahoma State to a 12–1 record in 2011. The Cowboys finished the season by rallying to beat Stanford 41–38 in overtime of a thrilling Fiesta Bowl.

In 2021, Gundy led another 12-win campaign. Once again, the Cowboys' season ended in a Fiesta Bowl comeback. This time they rallied from 28–7 down to beat Notre Dame 37–35. Oklahoma State reached bowl games in each of the next two seasons too. However, the team's streak of 18 consecutive winning seasons came to an end in 2024.

Oklahoma State quarterback Spencer Sanders (3) fires a pass during the Fiesta Bowl on January 1, 2022.

T. BOONE PICKENS

T. Boone Pickens graduated from Oklahoma A&M with a geology degree in 1951. After becoming wealthy in the oil industry, Pickens decided to give back to his school. He donated $165 million to the university's athletics programs in 2005. He specifically set aside $20 million to renovate Oklahoma State's football stadium. With the money, the school was able to turn Boone Pickens Stadium into a state-of-the-art facility.

FACT BOX

First Season: 1901

Location: Stillwater, Oklahoma

Stadium: Boone Pickens Stadium

Conference: Big 12 Conference

All-Time Record: 640–581–48

Bowl Record: 22–12

National Titles: 1945*

College Football Playoff Appearances: None

Top Coaches: Pappy Waldorf (1929–33); Jim Lookabaugh (1939–49); Mike Gundy (2005–)

Top Players: Bob Fenimore (1943–46); Neill Armstrong (1943–46); Leslie O'Neal (1982–85); Mark Moore (1983–86); Thurman Thomas (1984–87); Barry Sanders (1986–88); Dez Bryant (2007–09); Justin Blackmon (2009–11)

Mascot: Pistol Pete

*Title claimed by school, though not recognized by the NCAA.

OLE MISS REBELS

The University of Mississippi, known as Ole Miss, was a founding member of what is now the SEC in 1932. For years, the football team was among the conference's top contenders. The program's golden era came after the hiring of coach John Vaught in 1947. Over 25 seasons, Vaught put together 22 winning records. He also led the Rebels to SEC titles six times between 1947 and 1963.

In 1960, Ole Miss nearly completed a perfect season. The only setback was a 6–6 tie with rival LSU. But the team still claimed a share of the national title. Quarterback Jake Gibbs then finished off the 10–0–1 season by leading the team to a 14–6 win over Rice in the Sugar Bowl.

Vaught left after the 1970 season. By 1973, Ole Miss was struggling so much

A statue of John Vaught sits outside Ole Miss's Vaught-Hemingway Stadium in Oxford.

that the coach briefly returned for eight games. When Vaught retired for good after that, the Rebels slipped in the SEC standings. The team didn't start winning regularly again until the 1990s.

The Rebels got a boost in 2000 when Eli Manning arrived. By his senior year in 2003, the star quarterback led the Rebels to the Cotton Bowl. It was the team's first appearance in a major bowl game since 1969, when Eli's father, Archie Manning, was the team's signal-caller. Eli finished his college career by throwing two touchdown passes and rushing for another score as Ole Miss held off Oklahoma State to win 31–28.

Ole Miss quarterback Eli Manning led the SEC with 3,600 passing yards and 29 touchdowns in 2003.

The Rebels struggled for consistency after Manning graduated. But in 2024, coach Lane Kiffin led Ole Miss to its fifth consecutive bowl game. That was the longest streak since a run of 15 straight between the 1957 and 1971 seasons.

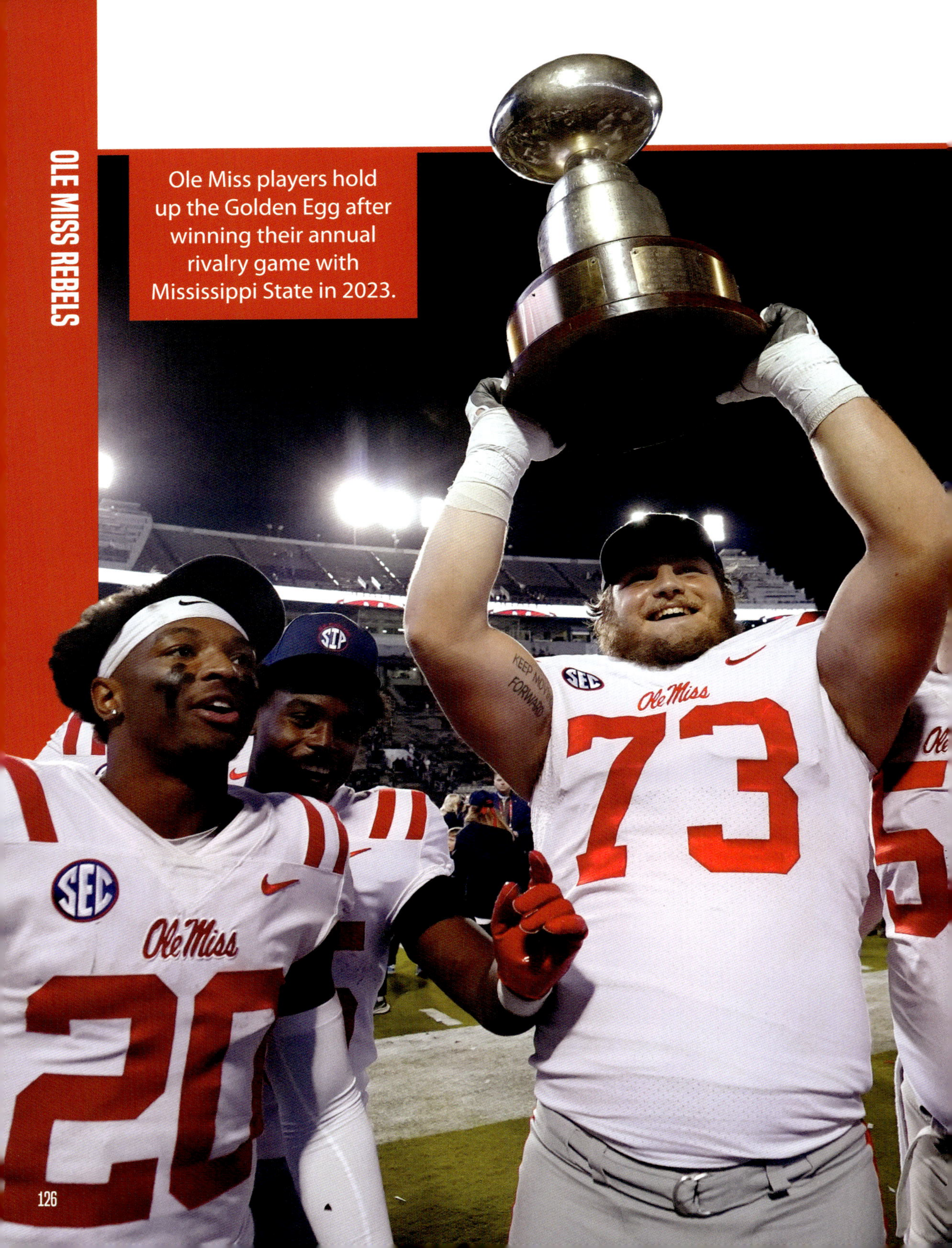

Ole Miss players hold up the Golden Egg after winning their annual rivalry game with Mississippi State in 2023.

THE EGG BOWL

The game Ole Miss fans look forward to the most each year is the annual end-of-season matchup against rival Mississippi State. The heated rivalry is known as the Egg Bowl for the golden egg-shaped trophy given to the winner. Ole Miss won the game for the 66th time in 121 meetings in 2024.

FACT BOX

First Season: 1893

Location: Oxford, Mississippi

Stadium: Vaught-Hemingway Stadium

Conference: Southeastern Conference

All-Time Record: 685–550–35

Bowl Record: 26–15

National Titles: 1959,* *1960*, 1962*

College Football Playoff Appearances: None

Top Coaches: John Vaught (1947–70, 1973); David Cutcliffe (1998–2004); Lane Kiffin (2021–)

Top Players: Frank Kinard (1935–37); Jake Gibbs (1958–60); Archie Manning (1968–70); Ben Williams (1972–75); Eli Manning (2000–03); Patrick Willis (2003–06); Michael Oher (2005–08); A. J. Brown (2016–18)

Mascot: Tony the Landshark

*Title claimed by school, though not recognized by the NCAA.

Shared National Titles in Italics

OREGON DUCKS

Oregon running back Ricky Whittle breaks a tackle during the Rose Bowl on January 2, 1995.

The Oregon football team was known as the Webfoots in its early days. Under that nickname, the team went to a pair of Rose Bowls after the 1916 and 1919 seasons. But the next seven decades were a struggle as Oregon appeared in only four bowl games. Between 1965 and 1986 the renamed Ducks had only four winning seasons.

Coach Rich Brooks began the program's turnaround in his final season when the Ducks made a surprise run to the Rose Bowl after the 1994 season. Brooks left the school soon after, but new coach Mike Bellotti helped turn Oregon into a yearly contender. Bellotti had only one losing record before leaving after the 2008 season.

His replacement, Chip Kelly, took Oregon to the BCS National Championship Game after the 2010 season. The Ducks lost to Auburn 22–19 on a late field goal. Oregon went back to the College Football Playoff Championship Game in 2014. That year, the team was led by Heisman Trophy–winning quarterback Marcus Mariota, who tossed 42 touchdowns

Quarterback Marcus Mariota became the all-time leading passer in Oregon history with 10,796 yards and 105 touchdowns.

and ran for 15 more. But Mariota's strong play wasn't enough, as the Ducks were beaten 42–20 by Ohio State in the title game.

While the Ducks were becoming a national power, they were also establishing a fashion trend in college football. After years of wearing green jerseys at home with yellow helmets, Oregon introduced a wide variety of uniform options. The team has consistently added new colors and patterns to its uniforms. Oregon has also alternated color combinations from week to week, creating a different look for each game.

Soon after Oregon started doing this, the idea spread. Other schools began to expand the variety of uniforms they used. Now many teams have several alternate uniform options to choose from throughout the season.

Oregon's football team has set itself apart for decades with its wide variety of uniform combinations.

A KNIGHT IN GREEN ARMOR

Oregon has long held a strong relationship with Nike. The athletic clothing company's main headquarters is in Beaverton, Oregon, just 107 miles (172 km) north of the university campus in Eugene. Nike founder Phil Knight graduated from Oregon in 1959. Over the years, Knight and his wife, Penny, have donated more than $1 billion to Oregon's athletic teams. The school has used the money to build a powerful sports program.

FACT BOX

First Season: 1894

Location: Eugene, Oregon

Stadium: Autzen Stadium

Conference: Big Ten Conference

All-Time Record: 718–512–46

Bowl Record: 17–21

National Titles: None

College Football Playoff Appearances: 2014, 2024

Top Coaches: Mike Bellotti (1995–2008); Chip Kelly (2009–12); Dan Lanning (2022–)

Top Players: Mel Renfro (1961–63); Bobby Moore (1969–71); Dan Fouts (1970–72); Haloti Ngata (2002–05); LaMichael James (2009–11); Marcus Mariota (2012–14); Royce Freeman (2014–17); Justin Herbert (2016–19); Penei Sewell (2018–19)

Mascot: The Duck

Penn State is located near the talent-rich region of western Pennsylvania. Football has been a huge part of the culture at the school since the team was founded in the late 1880s. But Penn State took a huge national leap forward when coach Joe Paterno was hired in 1966. The humble, quiet Paterno became beloved by fans as he put disciplined, winning teams on the field year after year.

Paterno coached Penn State's first Heisman winner, John Cappelletti, in 1973. Cappelletti was a talented running back. He accepted the award with a powerful speech honoring his brother, Joey, who was battling leukemia.

Penn State running back John Cappelletti rushed for more than 1,500 yards and 17 touchdowns in 1973.

Penn State players carry coach Joe Paterno off the field after beating the Miami Hurricanes 14–10 in the Fiesta Bowl in January 1987.

After years of close calls, Paterno delivered the school's first national title in 1982. The Nittany Lions capped the season by turning back a strong Georgia team 27–23 in the Sugar Bowl. After the 1986 season, Penn State took an 11–0 record into a national-title showdown with top-ranked Miami in the Fiesta Bowl. The Nittany Lions shut down the Hurricanes' high-powered passing attack with five interceptions in a 14–10 upset win.

In 2011, the program was rocked by an abuse scandal centered on longtime defensive coordinator Jerry Sandusky. Eventually, it was discovered that Paterno knew about Sandusky's actions. The beloved head coach was fired.

Penn State was put on probation and barred from playing in bowl games. Many top players left the school. New coach Bill O'Brien had to rebuild the program nearly from the ground up. James Franklin, who took over for O'Brien in 2014, completed the job by taking Penn State to the College Football Playoff semifinals in 2024.

Nittany Lions tight end Tyler Warren tries to make a move around a Notre Dame defender during a College Football Playoff game in January 2025.

THE WHITEOUT

Penn State was set to host Purdue in a 2004 game. In an effort to build more atmosphere at the 107,000-seat Beaver Stadium, school officials asked students to wear all white. Soon, "whiteout games" became a tradition several times per year. Home fans in the stadium wear white, creating an intimidating atmosphere for opponents.

FACT BOX

First Season: 1887

Location: University Park, Pennsylvania

Stadium: Beaver Stadium

Conference: Big Ten Conference

All-Time Record: 943–412–41

Bowl Record: 32–21–2

National Titles: 1982, 1986

College Football Playoff Appearances: 2024

Top Coaches: Rip Engle (1950–65); Joe Paterno (1966–2011); James Franklin (2014–)

Top Players: Ted Kwalick (1966–68); Jack Ham (1968–70); John Cappelletti (1971–73); Shane Conlan (1983–86); LaVar Arrington (1997–99); Paul Posluszny (2003–06); Saquon Barkley (2015–17); Micah Parsons (2018–19)

Mascot: Nittany Lion

PITTSBURGH PANTHERS

The Pittsburgh Panthers were one of college football's powerhouse teams in the early 1900s. Led by legendary coach Pop Warner, the school claimed three national titles in four years between 1915 and 1918, though the NCAA recognizes the Panthers winning only twice. Warner's teams of the era became known as "The Fighting Dentists" since many players became dentists or doctors after graduating.

Warner's replacement, Jock Sutherland, later found even more success. Sutherland never had a losing season between 1924 and 1938. In 1937, he and star running back Marshall Goldberg led the Panthers to a nearly perfect 9–0–1 season.

When Johnny Majors took over as head coach in 1973, the school hadn't had a winning season in ten years. But Majors led a dramatic turnaround. In 1976, the Panthers had their first Heisman Trophy winner in standout running back Tony Dorsett. Pittsburgh won all

Pittsburgh running back Marshall Goldberg earned All-America honors in both 1937 and 1938.

11 of its regular-season games by at least eight points. It then dismantled Georgia 27–3 in the Sugar Bowl. Dorsett rushed for 202 yards and a touchdown to secure the national title.

Majors left after the season, but new coach Jackie Sherrill kept the momentum going. The Panthers posted three straight 11–1 seasons between 1979 and 1981. Sherrill coached many future NFL stars, including defensive lineman Hugh Green and record-smashing quarterback Dan Marino.

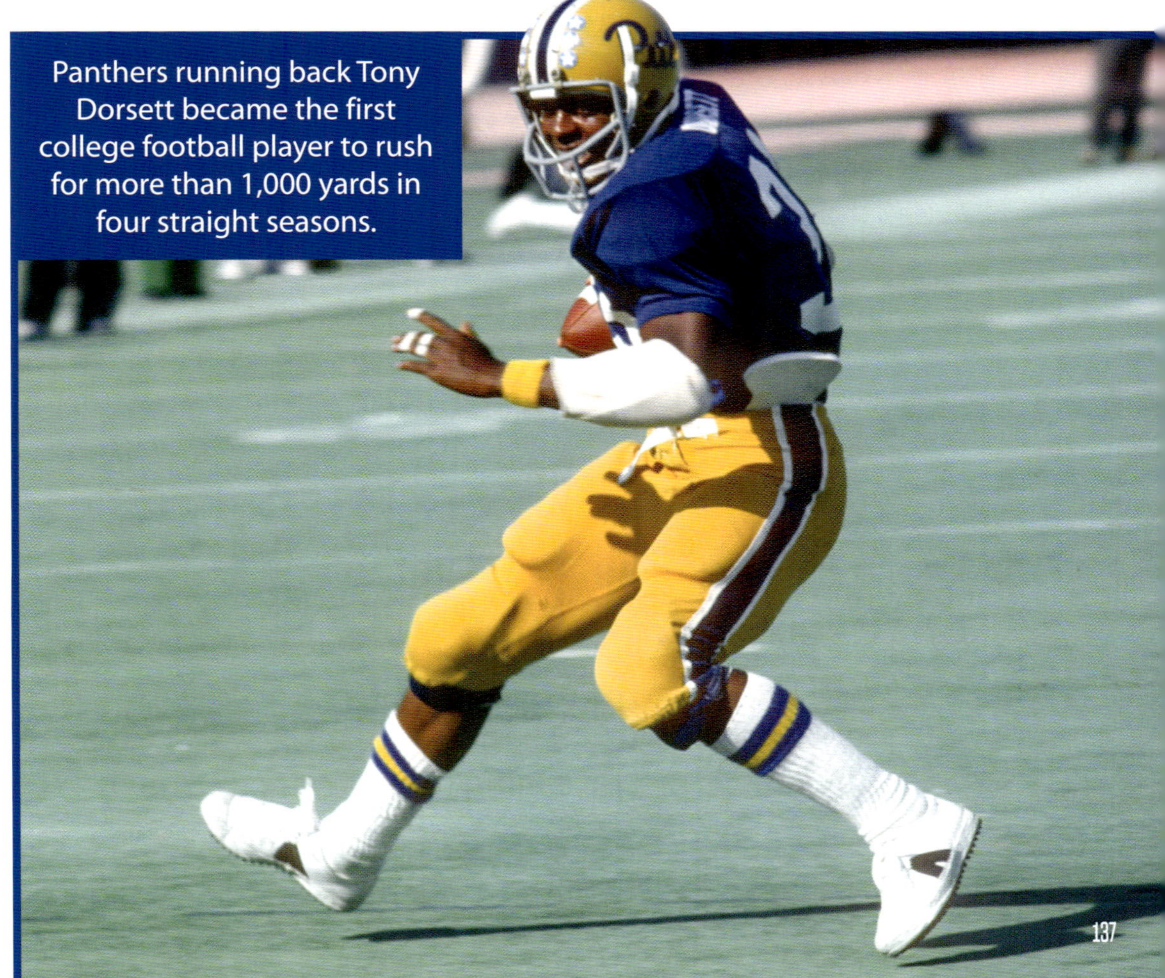

Panthers running back Tony Dorsett became the first college football player to rush for more than 1,000 yards in four straight seasons.

A TEAM OF FIRSTS

Pittsburgh has been involved in many college football broadcasting firsts. In 1921, a local radio station aired the first broadcast of a college game when Pittsburgh played West Virginia. When Pittsburgh played Duke in September 1951, NBC broadcast college football on nationwide TV for the first time. The Panthers were also featured in the first college football game broadcast on cable channel ESPN when they played BYU in September 1984.

Pittsburgh defensive lineman Hugh Green finished second in the Heisman Trophy voting in 1980. It was the highest finish for a defensive player at the time.

Pittsburgh didn't win 11 games again until the 2021 season. That year, quarterback Kenny Pickett threw 42 touchdown passes and led the team to an 11–2 record before the Panthers fell to Michigan State in the Peach Bowl. The quarterback broke many of the school's career passing records before being selected in the 2022 draft by the local Pittsburgh Steelers. Following a 3–7 season in 2023, the Panthers rebounded to 7–6 in 2024. It was the team's eighth winning record in ten seasons under coach Pat Narduzzi.

FACT BOX

First Season: 1890

Location: Pittsburgh, Pennsylvania

Stadium: Acrisure Stadium

Conference: Atlantic Coast Conference

All-Time Record: 768–566–42

Bowl Record: 15–23

National Titles: 1915,* 1916, *1918*, 1929,* 1931,* 1934,* 1936,* 1937, 1976

College Football Playoff Appearances: None

Top Coaches: Pop Warner (1915–23); Jock Sutherland (1924–38); Jackie Sherrill (1977–81)

Top Players: Robert Peck (1913–16); Marshall Goldberg (1936–38); Tony Dorsett (1973–76); Hugh Green (1977–80); Dan Marino (1979–82); Larry Fitzgerald (2002–03); Aaron Donald (2010–13); Kenny Pickett (2017–21)

Mascot: ROC the Panther

*Title claimed by school, though not recognized by the NCAA.

Shared National Titles in Italics

SYRACUSE ORANGE

Coach Ben Schwartzwalder, *right*, won 153 games at Syracuse from 1949 to 1973.

The Syracuse Orange have experienced several up-and-down swings in their football history. The biggest upswing came in 1959. That year, coach Ben Schwartzwalder's team shut out five opponents during an 11–0 season. The Orange were named national champions, then topped Texas 23–14 in the Cotton Bowl.

Schwartzwalder retired after the 1973 season. Finding a replacement proved difficult. In 1981, Dick MacPherson took over a struggling program and turned things around.

The Orange were 11–0 when they headed into the Sugar Bowl after the 1987 season. But a late Auburn field goal tied the game 16–16 and cost Syracuse another perfect season.

Paul Pasqualoni kept the team competitive in the 1990s, especially with the help of record-setting quarterback Donovan McNabb in the latter half of the decade. But the Orange struggled through the 2000s and 2010s. Between 2002 and 2017, the school never spent a single week in the top 25.

After leaving Syracuse, quarterback Donovan McNabb (5) was the No. 2 pick in the 1999 NFL Draft by the Philadelphia Eagles.

Syracuse has long been known for its excellent running backs. Jim Brown started the tradition in 1954. In three seasons with the school, he used his combination of speed and power to build a reputation as perhaps the finest college football player ever. Running back Ernie Davis

NO. 44

Wearing the No. 44 uniform at Syracuse was a special honor. Jim Brown first made the number famous during his career. Ernie Davis and Floyd Little also wore it. For years, the number was given to a deserving player. But the school decided to retire it for good in 2005. By then, the school had also changed its zip code from 13210 to 13244 to honor the uniform number.

Syracuse running back Jim Brown takes on a pair of Texas Christian defenders in the Cotton Bowl following the 1956 season.

starred on the school's 1959 championship team. Two years later, he became the first Black player to win the Heisman Trophy. Speedy back Floyd Little set new records for rushing yards and touchdowns before graduating in 1966.

In 1981, Joe Morris became the first Syracuse running back to break 4,000 career yards. His record still stood more than 40 years later. But Syracuse has also had strong backs in the 2000s. Walter Reyes set a new mark with 45 touchdowns between 2001 and 2004. Delone Carter broke the 3,000-yard mark before finishing his career in 2010. Sean Tucker topped 3,000 yards in just three seasons between 2020 and 2022.

FACT BOX

First Season: 1889

Location: Syracuse, New York

Stadium: JMA Wireless Dome

Conference: Atlantic Coast Conference

All-Time Record: 753–580–49

Bowl Record: 17–11–1

National Titles: 1959

College Football Playoff Appearances: None

Top Coaches: Frank "Buck" O'Neill (1906–07, 1913–15, 1917–19); Ben Schwartzwalder (1949–73); Paul Pasqualoni (1991–2004)

Top Players: Jim Brown (1954–56); Ernie Davis (1959–61); John Mackey (1960–62); Floyd Little (1964–66); Joe Morris (1978–81); Tim Green (1982–85); Don McPherson (1984–87); Donovan McNabb (1995–98); Dwight Freeney (1998–2001)

Mascot: Otto the Orange

TCU HORNED FROGS

The Texas Christian University (TCU) Horned Frogs were already a strong team when they joined the competitive Southwest Conference (SWC) in 1923. Over the next 20 seasons, TCU became a consistent national power. In the 1930s, two quarterbacks made the Horned Frogs nearly unbeatable. At the time, the forward pass was still a new concept in college football. Sammy Baugh helped make it a true weapon. In three seasons, he threw 587 passes and 39 touchdowns. Baugh led TCU to victory in the first Cotton Bowl after the 1936 season.

After Baugh left for the NFL, Davey O'Brien took over as quarterback for coach Dutch Meyer. In 1938, O'Brien led TCU to an 11–0 record. The Horned Frogs

TCU quarterback Davey O'Brien threw only four interceptions in 166 pass attempts during the 1938 season.

outscored their opponents 269–60. The team was named national champion. O'Brien, who threw 19 touchdown passes, became the first quarterback to win the Heisman Trophy.

Meyer left the team after the 1952 season. The Horned Frogs mostly struggled for the next four decades. When the SWC broke up in 1996, TCU's struggling team didn't join another major conference. Instead, the school joined the second-tier Western Athletic Conference.

In 1999, one of TCU's biggest stars burst into the spotlight. Junior running back LaDainian Tomlinson led the nation with 1,850 rushing yards. He piled up an NCAA-record 406 in

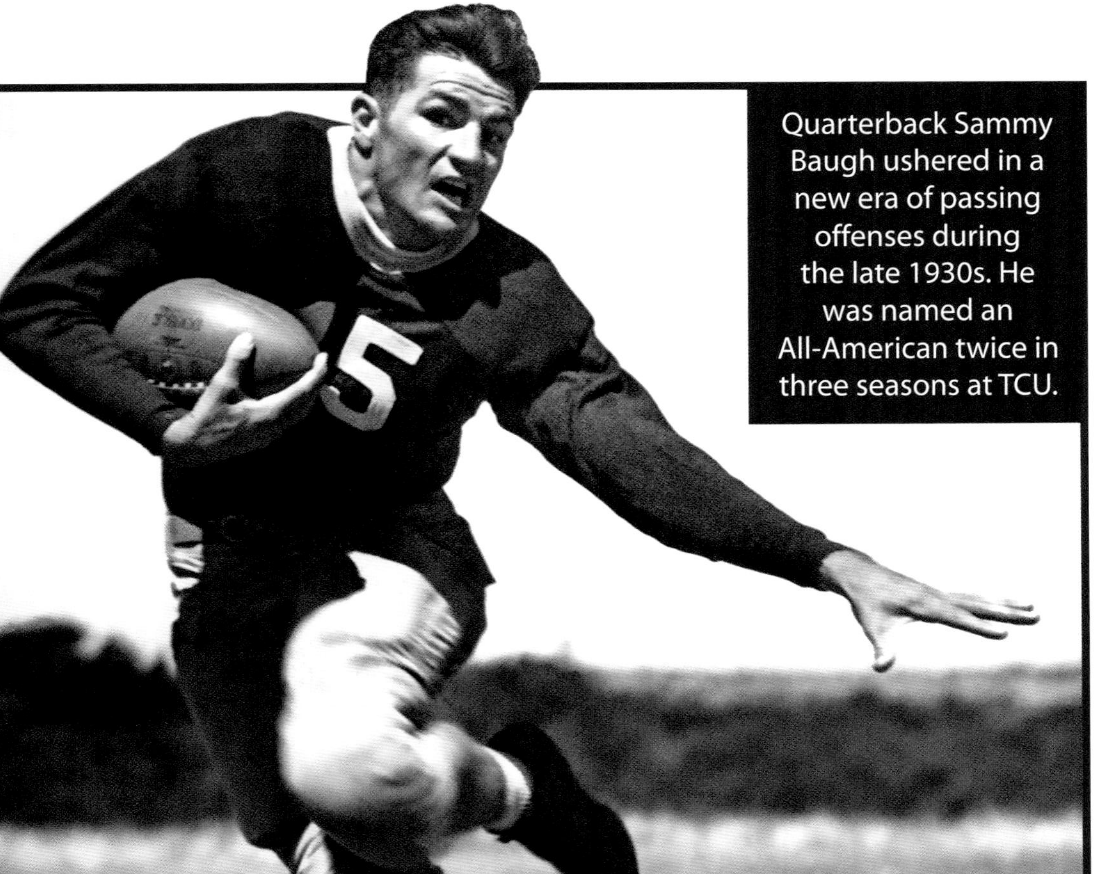

Quarterback Sammy Baugh ushered in a new era of passing offenses during the late 1930s. He was named an All-American twice in three seasons at TCU.

SOUTHWEST LEGACY

TCU developed some great rivalries during its 73 years in the SWC. Several went on hold when the conference broke up. However, some have since resumed. TCU and fellow Texas private school Baylor took a ten-year break before playing again in 2006. Since TCU joined the Big 12 in 2012, the teams now meet again each year. Fellow former SWC schools Houston, Oklahoma State, and Texas Tech were also in the Big 12 as of 2025.

Running back LaDainian Tomlinson set the TCU rushing record with 5,263 rushing yards from 1997 to 2000. He also ran for a record 54 touchdowns.

one game. As a senior in 2000, Tomlinson led the nation again with 2,158 rushing yards.

The Horned Frogs consistently improved throughout the 2000s under coach Gary Patterson. In 2012, the school was asked to join the Big 12. Patterson left the team during the 2021 season. But a year later, new coach Sonny Dykes took the Horned Frogs on a surprising run to the College Football Playoff. Star quarterback Max Duggan threw two touchdowns and rushed for two more in a 51–45 upset win over Michigan in the semifinals.

FACT BOX

First Season: 1896

Location: Fort Worth, Texas

Stadium: Amon G. Carter Stadium

Conference: Big 12 Conference

All-Time Record: 694–578–57

Bowl Record: 19–16–1

National Titles: 1935,* 1938

College Football Playoff Appearances: 2022

Top Coaches: Francis Schmidt (1929–33); Dutch Meyer (1934–52); Gary Patterson (2000–21)

Top Players: Sammy Baugh (1934–36); Davey O'Brien (1936–38); Jim Swink (1954–56); Kenneth Davis (1982–84); LaDainian Tomlinson (1997–2000); Andy Dalton (2007–10); Trevone Boykin (2012–15); Max Duggan (2019–22)

Mascot: SuperFrog

*Title claimed by school, though not recognized by the NCAA.

TENNESSEE VOLUNTEERS

The Tennessee Volunteers are famous for their many traditions. Those include their vivid orange uniforms, their famous "Rocky Top" fight song, and their familiar checkerboard-painted end zones. The team has been a powerhouse for more than a century.

The Volunteers' first great stretch came under coach Bob Neyland in the 1930s. In 1938, Neyland's team shut out seven of its ten regular-season opponents. The Volunteers then blanked No. 4 Oklahoma 17–0 in the Orange Bowl.

In addition to coaching at Tennessee for 21 seasons, Bob Neyland, *right*, was a brigadier general in the US Army.

Tennessee's Neyland Stadium holds 101,915 fans, making it the sixth-largest stadium in the country.

The following season, Tennessee didn't allow a single point in ten regular-season games. However, the Volunteers' streak of 15 straight shutouts came to an end in a shocking 14–0 Rose Bowl loss to USC.

Neyland's teams claimed national titles in 1938, 1940, and 1950. But the school's first NCAA-recognized championship came in 1951. Once again, the team was paced by its defense. The Volunteers shut out five of their ten opponents. They were named national champions before losing 28–13 to Maryland in the Sugar Bowl. Neyland coached one more year. In 1962, Tennessee named its home stadium after him.

THE VOL NAVY

Neyland Stadium sits on the banks of the Tennessee River. Many fans travel to games by boat. As many as 350 boats may dock near the stadium for big games. The floating fans are known as both the UT Armada and the Vol Navy.

Though Tennessee rarely had losing records, the team didn't compete for a national title until the late 1990s under coach Phillip Fulmer. Record-setting quarterback Peyton Manning got the Volunteers close to the top. But it was the year after Manning left when they finally put it all together. With quarterback Tee Martin under center in 1998, Tennessee beat five ranked teams to go 12–0.

Volunteers wide receiver Peerless Price breaks away for his 79-yard touchdown in the BCS National Championship Game in January 1999.

The Volunteers then took part in the first BCS National Championship Game against No. 2 Florida State. Martin hit wide receiver Peerless Price for a 79-yard touchdown catch with just over nine minutes left. It proved to be the key play in a 23–16 Fiesta Bowl win.

Tennessee struggled to compete with other SEC powers after Fulmer retired following the 2008 season. But the Volunteers came back under new coach Josh Heupel in the early 2020s. In 2022, he led Tennessee to its first 11-win season in more than two decades.

FACT BOX

First Season: 1891

Location: Knoxville, Tennessee

Stadium: Neyland Stadium

Conference: Southeastern Conference

All-Time Record: 875–417–53

Bowl Record: 30–25

National Titles: 1938,* 1940,* 1950,* 1951, 1967,* 1998

College Football Playoff Appearances: 2024

Top Coaches: Bob Neyland (1926–34, 1936–40, 1946–52); Johnny Majors (1977–92); Phillip Fulmer (1992–2008)

Top Players: George Cafego (1937–39); Bob Suffridge (1938–40); Doug Atkins (1950–52); Johnny Majors (1954–56); Reggie White (1980–83); Peyton Manning (1994–97); John Henderson (1999–2001); Eric Berry (2007–09)

Mascot: Smokey

*Title claimed by school, though not recognized by the NCAA.

TEXAS LONGHORNS

Texas defender George Brucks (66) tackles Navy quarterback Roger Staubach in the Cotton Bowl on January 1, 1964.

Texas first fielded a football team in 1893. The Longhorns were a powerhouse right away. The team didn't have a losing season until 1933.

Despite their early dominance, Texas didn't really take off until coach Darrell K Royal took over in 1957. He inherited a team that had finished 1–9 the year before. By 1963, Royal's Longhorns were No. 1 in the nation. They finished off an 11–0 season by routing No. 2 Navy 28–6 in the Cotton Bowl.

Texas was soon back on top. After famously rallying to beat rival Arkansas 15–14 in the final game of the 1969 regular season, the Longhorns went back to the Cotton Bowl to play Notre Dame. Texas went out on top after squeaking past the Fighting Irish 21–17.

One year later, Texas was 10–0 when the two teams met in a Cotton Bowl rematch. Though Notre Dame won the game, the Longhorns still finished No. 1 in the coaches' poll. Its voters had picked their champion prior to the game.

Despite having some strong teams through the 1980s, Texas fell short of another national championship. The team was drifting again when Mack Brown took over in 1998. Brown quickly built Texas back up, winning at least nine games in each of his first 12 seasons.

The best team during that run took the field in 2005. Led by electrifying quarterback Vince Young, the Longhorns averaged more than 50 points per game while finishing 12–0. That set up a much-hyped BCS Championship Game matchup with undefeated USC, which had won the previous two national titles.

Weeks earlier, Young had lost out on the Heisman Trophy to USC running back Reggie Bush.

Longhorns running back Ricky Williams won the Heisman Trophy in 1998 after rushing for 2,124 yards and 27 touchdowns.

BEVO

Texas is one of many schools with a live animal mascot. Bevo, a 1,700-pound (770-kg) longhorn steer, was introduced on Thanksgiving Day 1916. Bevo XV became the school's newest mascot in 2016.

Texas's dual-threat quarterback Vince Young threw for 267 yards while rushing for 200 yards and three touchdowns in the Rose Bowl against USC on January 4, 2006.

With 26 seconds remaining in the title game, Texas trailed 38–33 and faced fourth-and-five at the USC 9-yard line. Young scrambled right and raced to the end zone just ahead of the defense for a championship-clinching score. With that iconic play, Texas was back atop the college football world.

First Season: 1893

Location: Austin, Texas

Stadium: Darrell K Royal–Texas Memorial Stadium

Conference: Southeastern Conference

All-Time Record: 961–395–33

Bowl Record: 32–27–2

National Titles: 1963, 1969, *1970*, 2005

College Football Playoff Appearances: 2023, 2024

Top Coaches: Darrell K Royal (1957–76); Fred Akers (1977–86); Mack Brown (1998–2013)

Top Players: Bobby Layne (1944–47); Tommy Nobis (1963–65); Earl Campbell (1974–77); Ricky Williams (1995–98); Roy Williams (2000–03); Derrick Johnson (2001–04); Vince Young (2003–05); Colt McCoy (2006–09)

Mascot: Bevo

Shared National Titles in Italics

TEXAS A&M AGGIES

Texas A&M first rose to prominence in 1919. Coached that year by Dana X. Bible, the Aggies outscored their opponents 275–0. The dominant team wasn't named national champions at the time. But in 1980, the National Championship Foundation awarded Texas A&M, Notre Dame, and Harvard titles for that year.

Bible coached the Aggies successfully for a decade. In January 1922, he created one of the school's most legendary traditions. After a series of injuries in the Dixie Classic, Bible put a uniform on manager E. King Gill. Gill didn't end up playing in the game. But he became known as "The 12th Man." Soon, the student section began calling itself "The 12th Man."

Bible left Texas A&M after the 1928 season. In 1934, coach Homer Norton took over. By 1939, Norton had a powerful team. The Aggies allowed only 31 points all season. On offense, All-American running back John Kimbrough led the team

A banner at Kyle Field shows off Texas A&M's "12th Man" tradition.

Aggies running back John David Crow, *center*, poses with the Heisman Trophy after receiving the award in 1957.

THE 12TH MAN ON THE FIELD

In 1983, Texas A&M coach Jackie Sherrill put a new twist on the 12th Man tradition. He held open tryouts for walk-on players. Sherrill would then use those players to cover kickoffs. The school doesn't use the walk-on-only kickoff teams anymore. But one walk-on player is chosen as "The 12th Man" each season. The player is given jersey No. 12.

to an 11–0 finish and the national title.

Texas A&M has produced some great players. In 1957, two-way star John David Crow had 562 rushing yards and six touchdowns while throwing five touchdown passes. He also intercepted five passes while playing defensive back. His coach, Bear Bryant, said that if Crow didn't win the Heisman Trophy, the award should be discontinued. Ultimately, he did win.

The school's second Heisman winner was one of the most electrifying college football players ever. Johnny Manziel arrived in College Station in 2012. As a freshman, "Johnny Football" threw 26 touchdown passes. He also led the SEC

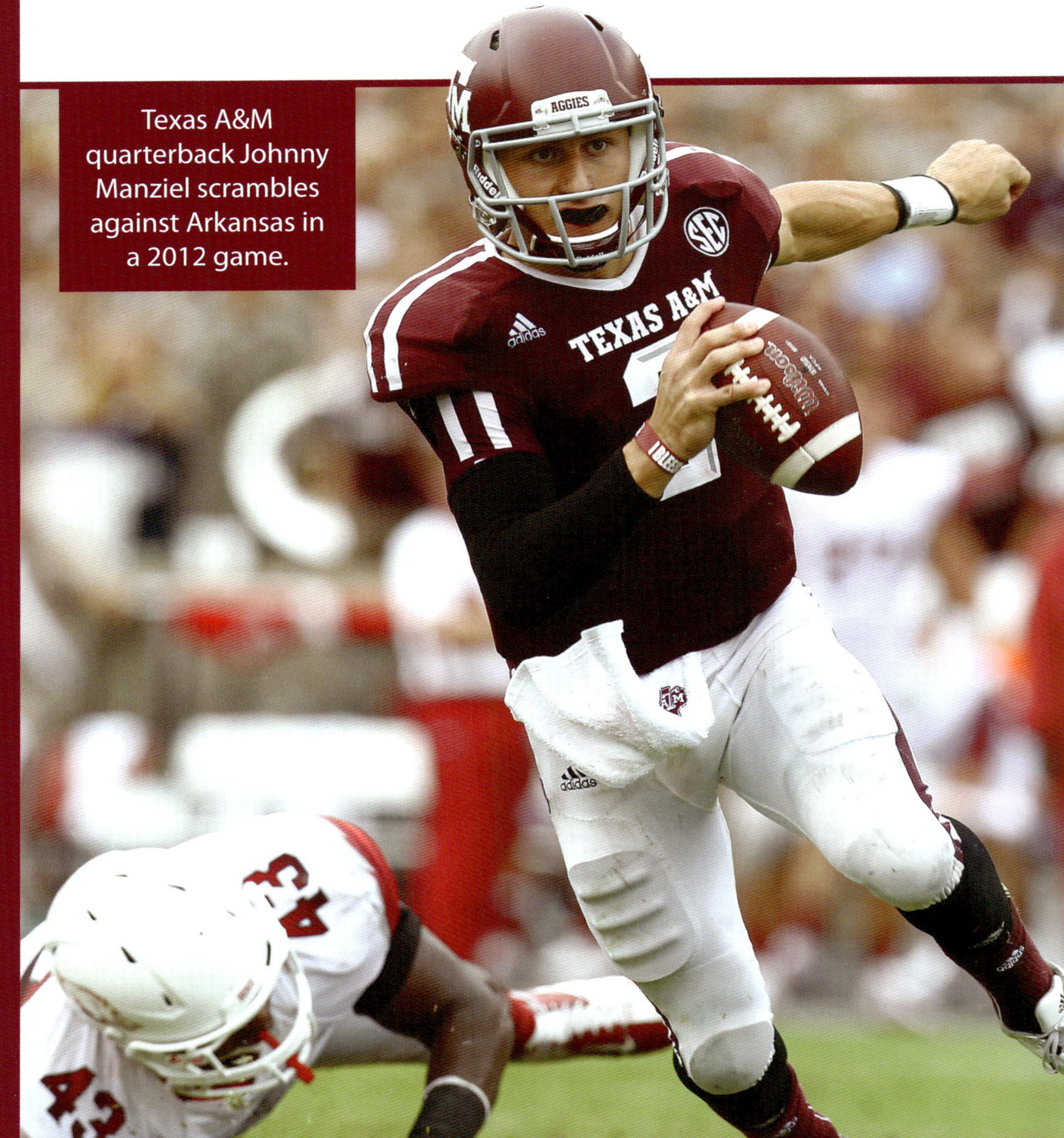

Texas A&M quarterback Johnny Manziel scrambles against Arkansas in a 2012 game.

with 1,410 rushing yards and 21 rushing touchdowns. That performance helped him become the first freshman to win the Heisman Trophy. He followed up that magical debut by throwing for more than 4,000 yards and 37 touchdowns as a sophomore. Manziel finished fifth in the Heisman voting before leaving for the NFL.

FACT BOX

First Season: 1894

Location: College Station, Texas

Stadium: Kyle Field

Conference: Southeastern Conference

All-Time Record: 786–509–48

Bowl Record: 20–24

National Titles: *1919*, 1927,* 1939

College Football Playoff Appearances: None

Top Coaches: Dana X. Bible (1917, 1919–28); Homer Norton (1934–47); R. C. Slocum (1989–2002)

Top Players: John Kimbrough (1938–40); John David Crow (1955–57); Johnny Holland (1983–86); Dat Nguyen (1995–98); Von Miller (2007–10); Mike Evans (2012–13); Johnny Manziel (2012–13); Myles Garrett (2014–16)

Mascot: Reveille

*Title claimed by school, though not recognized by the NCAA.

Shared National Titles in Italics

UCLA BRUINS

UCLA began playing its home games at the famous Rose Bowl in 1982. The stadium in Pasadena, California, is 25 miles (40 km) from UCLA's Westwood campus.

The University of California, Los Angeles (UCLA) began playing football in 1919. The Bruins joined the Pacific Coast Conference (PCC) in 1928. The conference grew and changed many times over the years before eventually turning into the Pac-12.

UCLA became one of the conference's top teams. Often, that meant a postseason trip to the Rose Bowl in nearby Pasadena, California. UCLA represented the conference in the glamorous bowl game after the 1942, 1946, and 1953 seasons.

In 1954, the Bruins finished the season 9–0 under coach Red Sanders. UCLA was named the national champion by the coaches' poll, one of the two major selectors. More than

70 years later, UCLA's 1954 squad still had the only unbeaten, untied record in school history. However, the team did not play in the Rose Bowl due to a PCC rule against teams going to the game in back-to-back years.

Despite two more Rose Bowl appearances after the 1955 and 1961 seasons, UCLA still hadn't won the game when it reached Pasadena again after the 1965 season. The Bruins faced No. 1 Michigan State, which was undefeated and had

In 1967, quarterback Gary Beban became the first UCLA player to win the Heisman Trophy.

beaten UCLA in the season opener. But behind star quarterback Gary Beban, UCLA built a 14–0 halftime lead and hung on for a dramatic 14–12 upset win.

UCLA has a long-standing rivalry with neighboring USC. The rivalry games were at their best in the late 1960s and early 1970s. Often, the game decided the conference championship. Between 1964 and 1979, the two schools won a combined total of 13 conference titles. Sanders once said that beating USC was more important than life and death. The heated rivalry continued even after both schools left the Pac-12 for the Big Ten in 2024.

Running back DeShaun Foster rushed for more than 3,000 yards and 39 touchdowns at UCLA between 1998 and 2001. In 2024, the Bruins hired Foster as head coach.

TRAILBLAZERS

Kenny Washington and Jackie Robinson were teammates in the UCLA backfield in 1939. After leaving UCLA, both became sports trailblazers. At the time, American professional sports leagues were segregated. Washington was one of four Black players to break pro football's color barrier in 1946. A year later, Robinson broke baseball's color barrier when he suited up for the Brooklyn Dodgers.

FACT BOX

First Season: 1919

Location: Los Angeles, California

Stadium: Rose Bowl

Conference: Big Ten Conference

All-Time Record: 642–453–37

Bowl Record: 17–20–1

National Titles: 1954

College Football Playoff Appearances: None

Top Coaches: Red Sanders (1949–57); Tommy Prothro (1965–70); Terry Donahue (1976–95)

Top Players: Kenny Washington (1937–39); Burr Baldwin (1941–42, 1946); Donn Moomaw (1950–52); Paul Cameron (1951–53); Gary Beban (1965–67); Kenny Easley (1977–80); Troy Aikman (1987–88); Jonathan Ogden (1992–95)

Mascot: Joe and Josephine Bruin

USC TROJANS

No school has produced as many Heisman Trophy winners as the University of Southern California (USC). Through the 2024 season, eight Trojans had won the award. And five of the eight were running backs. The school known as "Tailback U" has a long history of stars at the position.

The Trojans also have a winning tradition. USC played 102 seasons in some version of the Pac-12 Conference between 1922 and 2023. The team won the regular-season conference title 37 times. No other Pac-12 team has won more than 18. The school also lays claim to 11 national titles. USC's 36 bowl victories through 2024 ranked third all-time behind only Alabama and Georgia.

Running back Charles White won the Heisman Trophy in 1979. White is USC's all-time leading rusher with 5,598 yards.

The school's first great streak came under coach Howard Jones between 1925 and 1940. Jones's powerful teams were nicknamed "The Thundering Herd." He led the Trojans to four national titles.

Trojans running back Marcus Allen ran for 4,682 yards and 45 touchdowns from 1978 to 1981.

Coach John McKay was hired in 1960. In 16 years, his teams put together three undefeated seasons and had a winning record 14 years in a row. In 1965, running back Mike Garrett became the school's first Heisman Trophy winner. Another running back, O. J. Simpson, led the nation in rushing in both of his seasons at USC and won the Heisman in 1968.

After McKay left for the NFL, John Robinson took over. The Trojans won the 1978 national title, and Robinson coached two more Heisman winners in running backs Charles White and Marcus Allen. After the 1982 season, Robinson also left for the NFL, and the team struggled. So in the mid-1990s, Robinson came back. He led the team back to the Rose Bowl after the 1995 season.

By 2001, the Trojans were struggling. Pete Carroll took over as coach and put together a team of flashy, talented recruits. In a four-year stretch between 2002 and 2005, Carroll coached three Heisman winners. Two of them, quarterback Matt Leinart and running back

THE COMEBACK

USC trailed Notre Dame 24–0 late in the first half of the teams' 1974 rivalry game. Notre Dame had the top defense in the nation. But USC's powerful offense put on a stunning show starting late in the first half. In 17 minutes of game time, USC scored 55 points. The Trojans' 55–24 victory helped propel them to another national title.

Led by running back Reggie Bush (5) and quarterback Matt Leinart (11), the USC offense scored 1,030 total points between the 2003 and 2004 seasons.

Reggie Bush, led USC to back-to-back national titles in 2003 and 2004. However, the 2004 title was removed by the NCAA due to recruiting violations under Carroll. The scandal landed USC on probation. Twenty years later, the Trojans had put together some good seasons but were still trying to return to their previous heights.

FACT BOX

First Season: 1888

Location: Los Angeles, California

Stadium: Los Angeles Memorial Coliseum

Conference: Big Ten Conference

All-Time Record: 882–374–54

Bowl Record: 36–20

National Titles: 1928,* 1931, 1932, 1939,* 1962, 1967, 1972, *1974*, *1978*, *2003*, 2004*

College Football Playoff Appearances: None

Top Coaches: Howard Jones (1925–40); John McKay (1960–75); John Robinson (1976–82, 1993–97); Pete Carroll (2001–09)

Top Players: Mike Garrett (1963–65); O. J. Simpson (1967–68); Charles White (1976–79); Marcus Allen (1978–81); Carson Palmer (1998–2002); Matt Leinart (2003–05); Reggie Bush (2003–05); Caleb Williams (2022–23)

Mascot: Tommy Trojan, Traveler

*Title claimed by school, though not recognized by the NCAA.

Shared National Titles in Italics

UTAH UTES

The rivalry between Utah (in red) and BYU (in blue) is known as "The Holy War."

The Utah Utes spent more than a century playing in small conferences. Few outside of the state noticed the small but successful program. Utah's main source of recognition came as a fierce rival to neighboring BYU.

In the 2000s, while playing in the Mountain West, Utah became one of the top teams not playing in a major conference. That showed in 2004. Behind coach Urban Meyer and quarterback Alex Smith, the Utes went 11–0 in the regular season. Smith finished fourth in voting for the Heisman Trophy. Despite Utah's success, the BCS passed over the Utes for the national championship game. Instead, Utah blew out

Pittsburgh in the Fiesta Bowl. Smith threw four touchdown passes and rushed for a team-high 68 yards in a 35–7 win.

Meyer left for Florida after the season, and assistant Kyle Whittingham took over. The Utes continued to disrupt the college football world. In 2008, Utah finished the regular season 12–0. The record included wins over Michigan and Oregon State, as well as ranked opponents TCU and BYU. However, once again the undefeated Utes were passed over for a shot at the BCS title game.

It was a controversial decision, since finalists Florida and Oklahoma both had one loss. Utah instead went to the Sugar Bowl and topped favored

Utah quarterback Alex Smith threw 32 touchdowns and only four interceptions during his senior season in 2004.

Alabama 31–17. The Utes finished the season as the only undefeated team in the nation.

Utah's days as an underdog came to an end when the school joined the Pac-12 in 2011. Over 12 years in the powerhouse conference, Whittingham's teams won at least ten games four times. When the Pac-12 broke up after the 2023 season, Utah joined the Big 12.

Utah wide receiver David Reed reaches for a catch against Alabama in the Sugar Bowl on January 2, 2009.

THE MUSS

Founded in 2002, the Utah student section is known as "The MUSS." The name comes from a lyric in the school's fight song: "No rival band of college fans / dare meet us in the muss." Muss has become an acronym that means "Mighty Utah Student Section." The MUSS's 8,000 fans traditionally stand for the entire game.

FACT BOX

First Season: 1892

Location: Salt Lake City, Utah

Stadium: Rice-Eccles Stadium

Conference: Big 12 Conference

All-Time Record: 724–489–31

Bowl Record: 17–9

National Titles: None

College Football Playoff Appearances: None

Top Coaches: Ike Armstrong (1925–49); Ron McBride (1990–2002); Urban Meyer (2003–04); Kyle Whittingham (2004–)

Top Players: Larry Wilson (1957–59); Bryan Rowley (1989–93); Luther Elliss (1991–94); Jordan Gross (1999–2002); Alex Smith (2002–04); Eric Weddle (2003–06); Star Lotulelei (2010–12); Zack Moss (2016–19)

Mascot: Swoop

VIRGINIA TECH HOKIES

Formed in 1892, Virginia Tech's football program enjoyed a solid first century. The team frequently posted winning records in the Southern Conference from 1921 to 1964, and then as an independent after that. However, the Hokies were rarely ranked in the polls. They didn't win a bowl game until the 1986 season.

The golden era for the program began the next year, when Frank Beamer took over as coach. A former star defensive back for the Hokies, Beamer needed some time to settle in to his

The Virginia Tech players take the field to Metallica's "Enter Sandman" ahead of home games at Lane Stadium.

new role. But after Virginia Tech joined the Big East Conference in 1991, the Hokies began to take off.

Virginia Tech's first breakthrough came in 1995. The team capped off a 10–2 season with a 28–10 win over Texas in the Sugar Bowl. It was the Hokies' first win in a major bowl game.

Beamer's teams were known for tough defense and terrific special teams. In Beamer's 29 seasons, Virginia Tech blocked 136 kicks. The Hokies also scored 55 touchdowns on special teams. Their style of play was known as "Beamer Ball."

Beamer's best season came in 1999. Led by lightning-fast dual-threat quarterback Michael Vick, the Hokies started 7–0. Playing on the road the next week, the Hokies trailed West Virginia 20–19 with 1:15 left. Then Vick led a drive to set up a game-winning

Hokies quarterback Michael Vick finished third in the Heisman Trophy voting after the 1999 season.

The Hokies carry coach Frank Beamer off the field after beating Virginia in 2015, which was Beamer's final season with the team.

HOKIES OR GOBBLERS?

Virginia Tech's original nickname was the Gobblers. The team even had a live turkey mascot at games. But in the 1980s, coach Bill Dooley wanted to change the name to something tougher. Virginia Tech went with Hokies. The name originated from a cheer dating back to 1896. A Hokie is described as any loyal Virginia Tech fan.

44-yard field goal from kicker Shayne Graham. "The Miracle in Morgantown" drove the Hokies on to an 11–0 record and a spot in the national championship game. The dream ended there with a 46–29 loss to Florida State.

Beamer left Virginia Tech after the 2015 season. His 238 wins were nearly 200 more than any other coach in school history. He also owned 11 of the team's 14 bowl victories. In 2018, the school placed a statue of Beamer outside of Lane Stadium.

FACT BOX

First Season: 1892

Location: Blacksburg, Virginia

Stadium: Lane Stadium

Conference: Atlantic Coast Conference

All-Time Record: 778–512–46

Bowl Record: 14–22

National Titles: None

College Football Playoff Appearances: None

Top Coaches: Jerry Claiborne (1961–70); Bill Dooley (1978–86); Frank Beamer (1987–2015)

Top Players: Carroll Dale (1956–59); Frank Loria (1965–67); Frank Beamer (1966–68); Bruce Smith (1981–84); Jim Pyne (1990–93); Cornell Brown (1993–96); Corey Moore (1997–99); Michael Vick (1999–2000)

Mascot: HokieBird

WASHINGTON HUSKIES

Washington running back Hugh McElhenny scores a touchdown against Montana during a 1951 game.

After originally being known as the Sun Dodgers and the Vikings, Washington adopted the Huskies nickname in 1922. The following season, Washington played in the first of two Rose Bowls in three years. But the Huskies didn't win the prestigious game until their fourth try. After a 9–1 season in 1959, coach Jim Owens's team routed Wisconsin 44–8 in the iconic bowl game in Pasadena, California.

For the next two decades, Washington took a back seat to powerhouses UCLA and USC in what was then known as the Pac-8 Conference. Owens left in 1975 after back-to-back losing seasons. New coach Don James slowly turned things around.

With help from star quarterback Warren Moon, Washington won its first conference title in 14 years after the 1977 season.

James coached Washington for 18 years. In that stretch, his teams won at least ten games five times. The Huskies' finest season came in 1991. Quarterback Billy Joe Hobert threw a Pac-10-leading 22 touchdown passes. Star receiver Mario Bailey led the team with 17 touchdown catches. Meanwhile, defensive tackle Steve Emtman anchored a stellar defense that ranked second in the nation. Washington won all but one of its conference games by at least 11 points and rolled into the Rose Bowl with an 11–0 record. Facing Michigan, the Huskies put together a dominating

Quarterback Billy Joe Hobert threw two touchdown passes in Washington's Rose Bowl win over Michigan in January 1992.

second half to win 34–14. After the season, Washington shared the national title with Miami.

James left a year later as the school's all-time wins leader. For the next three decades, several coaches struggled to get Washington back on top. In 2023, Kalen DeBoer led the Huskies to the College Football Playoff championship game. Despite a heroic effort from quarterback Michael Penix Jr., the Heisman Trophy runner-up, the Huskies fell 34–13 to Michigan.

Huskies quarterback Michael Penix Jr. led the nation with 4,903 passing yards in 2023.

THE APPLE CUP

Since 1900, Washington's biggest rivalry game has been with cross-state foe Washington State. The game became known as the Apple Cup in 1962 since the state produces so much of this popular fruit. In 2023, the Huskies won the rivalry game for a 73rd time. Although Washington left for the Big Ten in 2024, the schools planned to continue the Apple Cup.

FACT BOX

First Season: 1889

Location: Seattle, Washington

Stadium: Husky Stadium

Conference: Big Ten Conference

All-Time Record: 781–473–50

Bowl Record: 21–22–1

National Titles: 1991

College Football Playoff Appearances: 2016, 2023

Top Coaches: Enoch Bagshaw (1921–29); Don James (1975–92); Kalen DeBoer (2022–23)

Top Players: George Wilson (1923–25); Chuck Carroll (1926–28); Hugh McElhenny (1949–51); Warren Moon (1975–77); Steve Emtman (1989–91); Napoleon Kaufman (1991–94); Marques Tuiasosopo (1997–2000); Michael Penix Jr. (2022–23)

Mascot: Dubs, Harry the Husky

WISCONSIN BADGERS

Wisconsin began playing football in 1889. It took more than a century for the Badgers to become a consistently successful team. But even some of Wisconsin's losses were thrilling. On January 1, 1963, the Badgers trailed USC 42–14 early in the fourth quarter of the Rose Bowl. Then Wisconsin quarterback Ron Vander Kelen led a furious rally before the Badgers ultimately fell short in a 42–37 loss.

Wisconsin finally won a bowl game for the first time after the 1982 season. But when new coach Barry Alvarez arrived in 1990, the program was struggling. The team got even worse in Alvarez's first season, finishing 1–10. Then the Badgers got

Wisconsin has played in Camp Randall Stadium since 1917. Prior to being a stadium, the site was used to train Union soldiers during the American Civil War (1861–65).

Wisconsin running back Brent Moss scores a touchdown against UCLA in the Rose Bowl on January 1, 1994.

a lot better. With an offense built behind a strong line and powerful running backs, the Badgers returned to the Rose Bowl after the 1993 season. A 21–16 win over UCLA capped a 10–1–1 season and gave the Badgers their first Rose Bowl victory.

Wisconsin remained competitive with Alvarez manning the sideline through 2005. In the years that followed, coaches Bret Bielema, Gary Andersen, Paul Chryst, and Luke Fickell have kept that streak going. Wisconsin missed a bowl game in 2024 for the first time in 23 years. That had been the third-longest active streak in the nation.

Wisconsin running back Ron Dayne rushed for 1,834 yards and 19 touchdowns in his Heisman Trophy–winning 1999 season.

JUMP AROUND

At the end of the third quarter of each game at Wisconsin's Camp Randall Stadium, the Badgers play the 1992 House of Pain song "Jump Around." Students jump in place as they dance to the song. The tradition began in 1998. In 2003, the school worried the jumping might damage the stadium. The administration briefly canceled the new tradition. After students protested, engineers were brought in for tests. They decided that the dancing posed no harm, and the tradition resumed.

Wisconsin's tradition of great running backs predated Alvarez. Alan Ameche won the school's first Heisman Trophy in 1954. "The Iron Horse" played both offense and defense. He ran for nine touchdowns that season. Ron Dayne won the Heisman in 1999. The powerful back finished that season as the NCAA's all-time leading rusher with 6,397 yards. In the 2000s, both Montee Ball and Jonathan Taylor cracked 5,000 yards in their careers. That made Wisconsin the only school with three 5,000-yard rushers in its history.

FACT BOX

First Season: 1889

Location: Madison, Wisconsin

Stadium: Camp Randall Stadium

Conference: Big Ten Conference

All-Time Record: 747–525–53

Bowl Record: 19–15

National Titles: None

College Football Playoff Appearances: None

Top Coaches: Phil King (1896–1902, 1905); Barry Alvarez (1990–2005, 2012, 2014); Bret Bielema (2006–12)

Top Players: Dave Schreiner (1940–42); Alan Ameche (1951–54); Pat Richter (1960–62); Ron Dayne (1996–99); Lee Evans (1999–2003); Joe Thomas (2003–06); Montee Ball (2009–12); Jonathan Taylor (2017–19)

Mascot: Bucky Badger

ALL-TIME FBS RECORDS

CAREER RECORDS

Passing Yards
Case Keenum, Houston (2007–11): 19,217

Passing Touchdowns
Case Keenum, Houston (2007–11): 155
Dillon Gabriel, Central Florida, Oklahoma, Oregon (2019–24): 155

Rushing Yards
Donnel Pumphrey, San Diego State (2013–16): 6,405

Rushing Touchdowns
Keenan Reynolds, Navy (2012–15): 88

Receptions
Zay Jones, East Carolina (2013–16): 399

Receiving Yards
Corey Davis, Western Michigan (2013–16): 5,285

Receiving Touchdowns
Jarett Dillard, Rice (2005–08): 60

Total Yards
Case Keenum, Houston (2007–11): 20,114

Tackles
Carlton Martial, Troy (2018–22): 577

Sacks
Jaylon Ferguson, Louisiana Tech (2015–18): 45

Interceptions
Al Brosky, Illinois (1950–52): 29

Field Goals Made
Christopher Dunn, North Carolina State (2018–22): 97

Scoring
Will Reichard, Alabama (2019–23): 547

SINGLE-SEASON RECORDS

Passing Yards
Bailey Zappe, Western Kentucky (2021): 5,967

Passing Touchdowns
Bailey Zappe, Western Kentucky (2021): 62

Rushing Yards
Barry Sanders, Oklahoma State (1988): 2,628

Rushing Touchdowns
Barry Sanders, Oklahoma State (1988): 37

Receptions
Zay Jones, East Carolina (2016): 158

Receiving Yards
Trevor Insley, Nevada (1999): 2,060

Receiving Touchdowns
Troy Edwards, Louisiana Tech (1998): 27

Total Yards
Joe Burrow, LSU (2019): 6,039

Tackles
Luke Kuechly, Boston College (2011): 191

Sacks
Terrell Suggs, Arizona State (2002): 24

Interceptions
Al Worley, Washington (1968): 14
Gerod Holliman, Louisville (2014): 14

Field Goals Made
Billy Bennett, Georgia (2003): 31

Scoring
Montee Ball, Wisconsin (2011): 236

SINGLE-GAME RECORDS

Passing Yards
Connor Halliday, Washington State (October 4, 2014): 734
Patrick Mahomes, Texas Tech (October 22, 2016): 734

Passing Touchdowns
David Klingler, Houston (November 17, 1990): 11

Rushing Yards
Samaje Perine, Oklahoma (November 22, 2014): 427

Rushing Touchdowns
Howard Griffith, Illinois (September 22, 1990): 8
Kalen Ballage, Arizona State (September 11, 2016): 8
Jaret Patterson, Buffalo (November 28, 2020): 8

Receptions
Randy Gatewood, UNLV (September 17, 1994): 23
Tyler Jones, Eastern Michigan (November 28, 2008): 23

Receiving Yards
Troy Edwards, Louisiana Tech (August 29, 1998): 405

Receiving Touchdowns
Rashaun Woods, Oklahoma State (September 20, 2003): 7

Total Yards
Patrick Mahomes, Texas Tech (October 22, 2016): 819

Tackles
Kenneth Murray, Oklahoma (September 22, 2018): 28

Sacks
Ameer Ismail, Western Michigan (October 21, 2006): 6
Elvis Dumervil, Louisville (September 4, 2005): 6
Ivan Pace Jr., Miami (Ohio) (November 12, 2019): 6

Interceptions
Lee Cook, Oklahoma State (November 28, 1942): 5
Walt Pastuszak, Brown (October 8, 1949): 5
Byron Beaver, Houston (September 22, 1962): 5
Dan Rebsch, Miami (Ohio) (November 4, 1972): 5

Field Goals Made
Mike Prindle, Western Michigan (September 29, 1984): 7
Dale Klein, Nebraska (October 19, 1985): 7

Scoring
Howard Griffith, Illinois (September 22, 1990): 48
Kalen Ballage, Arizona State (September 10, 2016): 48
Jaret Patterson, Buffalo (November 28, 2020): 48

GLOSSARY

campus
The grounds of a school.

dual-threat
Very good at two different skills, such as passing and running.

electrolytes
Substances that help a person's body create chemical reactions.

favorite
The person or team that is expected to win.

Hail Mary
A long pass that has a small chance of succeeding, usually made near the end of a game as a last-ditch effort to score.

iconic
Well-known for excellence.

junior college
A two-year college that often includes athletic programs.

lore
Historic traditions that are celebrated by a group.

option
A style of offense or a particular play in which the quarterback can either hand the ball off, carry it himself, pitch it back to another player, or drop back to pass.

overtime
An extra period of play when the score is tied after regulation.

poll
A survey of opinions on a subject. In college football, polls are used to rank teams from across the country.

prestigious
Highly thought of.

probation
Being subject to strict rules and regulations as a punishment for breaking the rules.

recruiting
Persuading a high school player to attend a certain college, usually to play sports.

rival
An opponent with whom a player or team has a fierce and ongoing competition.

segregated
Separated based on race, gender, ethnicity, or other factors.

upset
To unexpectedly beat a team that was heavily favored to win, or a game in which the heavily favored team loses.

walk-on
A college athlete who does not have a scholarship.

TO LEARN MORE

FURTHER READINGS

Ellis, Abigail, ed. *Illustrated Sports Encyclopedia*. DK Penguin Random House, 2023.

Hanlon, Luke. *Football Strategies*. Abdo, 2024.

Stathes, Corbu. *Everything Football*. Abdo, 2024.

ONLINE RESOURCES

To learn more about college football, please visit **abdobooklinks.com** or scan this QR code. These links are routinely monitored and updated to provide the most current information available.

INDEX

PHOTO CREDITS

Cover Photos: Joey Sussman/Shutterstock Images, front (trophy); Samuel Lewis/Corbis/Icon Sportswire/Getty Images, front (Tim Tebow); Otto Greule Jr./Getty Images Sport/Getty Images, front (Marcus Mariota); John E. Moore III/Getty Images Sport/Getty Images, front (Travis Hunter); Damien Strohmeyer/Allsport/Hulton Archive/Getty Images, front (Bo Jackson); Sporting News/Getty Images, front (Peyton Manning); Kevin C. Cox/Getty Images Sport/Getty Images, front (Jayden Daniels); Shutterstock Images, back (Heisman Trophy); Bettmann/Getty Images, back (Jim Brown)

Interior Photos: John Raoux/AP Images, 1, 52; Joe Robbins/Icon Sportswire/Getty Images, 2–3, 26–27; Wikimedia Commons, 4; Hum Historical/Alamy, 5; Corbis Historical/Getty Images, 6; AP Images, 7, 8–9, 50, 98–99 (left), 103, 106–107, 112, 117, 148, 152, 157, 165; Bettmann/Getty Images, 9, 66, 94, 136–137, 142, 144; Bob Riha Jr./Archive Photos/Getty Images, 10–11, 24; Focus On Sport/Getty Images, 12, 20, 59, 108; Hans Deryk/AP Images, 14; Jed Jacobsohn/Getty Images Sport/Getty Images, 15; Nam Y. Huh/AP Images, 16; Todd Kirkland/Getty Images Sport/Getty Images, 18–19, 19; Scott Cunningham/Getty Images Sport/Getty Images, 21; Kevin C. Cox/Getty Images Sport/Getty Images, 22, 30–31; Jed Jacobsohn/Allsport/Getty Images Sport/Getty Images, 25; Mike Zarrilli/Getty Images Sport/Getty Images, 28; Damien Strohmeyer/Allsport/Hulton Archive/Getty Images, 29; Dave Martin/AP Images, 32–33, 83; Jonathan Ferrey/Getty Images Sport/Getty Images, 34–35; Steve Grayson/WireImage/Getty Images, 35; Steve Conner/AP Images, 36; Kevin Reece/Getty Images Sport/Getty Images, 38; Chris Gardner/Getty Images Sport/Getty Images, 39, 168; Mike Powell/Allsport/Hulton Archive/Getty Images, 40–41; Steve Jacobson/IOS/AP Images, 42; John Byrum/Icon Sportswire, 43; Streeter Lecka/Getty Images Sport/Getty Images, 45; Andrew Wevers/Getty Images Sport/Getty Images, 46–47; Ray Fairall/AP Images, 47; Mario Cantu/Cal Sport Media/AP Images, 48–49; Brian Bahr/Getty Images Sport/Getty Images, 51, 67; Doug Mills/AP Images, 54–55; Doug Benc/Getty Images Sport/Getty Images, 55; Doug Benc/AP Images, 56–57; Frank Filan/AP Images, 58; Brian Rothmuller/Icon Sportswire/Getty Images, 60; John Amis/AP Images, 62–63; Scott Halleran/Getty Images Sport/Getty Images, 63; Marc Serota/Getty Images Sport/Getty Images, 64–65; Michael Hickey/Getty Images Sport/Getty Images, 68–69, 80–81; University of Iowa/WireImage/Getty Images, 70–71; Bernstein Associates/Getty Images Sport/Getty Images, 71, 177; Bailey Hillesheim/Icon Sportswire/Getty Images, 72–73; Earl Richardson/Allsport/Getty Images Sport/Getty Images, 74; Todd Warshaw/Getty Images Sport/Getty Images, 75; Peter Aiken/WireImage/Getty Images, 76; George Gojkovich/Getty Images Sport/Getty Images, 78, 137, 138; Matthew Stockman/Getty Images Sport/Getty Images, 78–79; Jacob Harris/AP Images, 82; Aaron M. Sprecher/AP Images, 84, 186–187; Joe Sebo/AP Images, 86; Kathy Willens/AP Images, 87; Harry How/Getty Images Sport/Getty Images, 88–89; Shutterstock Images, 90; Doug Sheridan/AP Images, 91; Karen Warren/Houston Chronicle/Hearst Newspapers/Getty Images, 92–93, 158–159; Rich Clarkson/NCAA Photos/Getty Images, 95, 161; Robert Gauthier/Los Angeles Times/Getty Images, 97; CEK/AP Images, 98–99 (right); Dylan Buell/Getty Images Sport/Getty Images, 100–101; Dave Weaver/AP Images, 102–103; Albert Dickson/Sporting News Archive/Getty Images, 104–105; John Byrum/Icon Sportswire/Getty Images, 107; Fred Kfoury III/Icon Sportswire/Getty Images, 110–111; Roger Wimmer/ISI Photos/Getty Images Sport/Getty Images, 110; Ric Tapia/AP Images, 112–113; Rich von Biberstein/Icon Sportswire/Getty Images, 114; Harold Valentine/AP Images, 116–117; Eliot J. Schechter/Allsport/Getty Images Sport/Getty Images, 118; Gary Siegel/Cal Sport Media/ZUMA Wire/AP Images, 120–121 (left); David Longstreath/AP Images, 120–121 (right), 184; Brandon Sloter/AP Images, 122; Wesley Hitt/Getty Images Sport/Getty Images, 124; Sporting News Archive/Getty Images, 125; Rogelio V. Solis/AP Images, 126–127; Mike Powell/Allsport/Getty Images Sport/Getty Images, 128; Craig Mitchelldyer/Getty Images Sport/Getty Images, 129; Sean M. Haffey/Getty Images Sport/Getty Images, 130–131; Paul Vathis/AP Images, 132; Jim Gerberich/AP Images, 133; Peter Joneleit/Icon Sportswire/Getty Images, 134–135; Anthony Camerano/AP Images, 140; Vincent Laforet/Hulton Archive/Getty Images, 141; JFL/AP Images, 145; Ronald Martinez/Getty Images Sport/Getty Images, 146; Doug Pensinger/Getty Images Sport/Getty Images, 148–149; Brad Mangin/Sports Illustrated/Getty Images, 150; Eric Gay/AP Images, 153; Lenny Ignelzi/AP Images, 154–155; Daniel Dunn/Icon Sportswire/Getty Images, 156; Kirby Lee/AP Images, 160; Vince Compagnone/Los Angeles Times/Getty Images, 162–163; Wally Fong/AP Images, 164–165; Kevork Djansezian/AP Images, 166, 182; George Frey/Getty Images Sport/Getty Images, 169; Alex Brandon/AP Images, 170; Doug Pensinger/Allsport/Getty Images Sport/Getty Images, 172; Al Messerschmidt Archive/AP Images, 173; Steve Helber/AP Images, 174; Gene Herrick/AP Images, 176; Nick Tre. Smith/Icon Sportswire/Getty Images, 178–179; David Stluka/AP Images, 180–181; Stephen Dunn/Allsport/Getty Images Sport/Getty Images, 181

ABDOBOOKS.COM
Published by Abdo Reference, a division of ABDO, PO Box 398166, Minneapolis, Minnesota 55439.

Printed in China.
102025
012026

Editor: Chrös McDougall
Series Designer: Colleen McLaren
Production Designer: Kate Liestman

LIBRARY OF CONGRESS CONTROL NUMBER: 2025939305

PUBLISHER'S CATALOGING-IN-PUBLICATION DATA
Names: Beattie, Charlie, author.
Title: The college football encyclopedia / by Charlie Beattie
Description: Minneapolis, Minnesota: Abdo Reference, 2026 | Series: College sports encyclopedias | Includes online resources and index.
Identifiers: ISBN 9781098298838 (lib. bdg.) | ISBN 9798384932635 (ebook)
Subjects: LCSH: American football--Juvenile literature. | College sports--Juvenile literature. | Football--Records--United States--Juvenile literature. | Football teams--Juvenile literature. | Sports--United States--History--Juvenile literature. | Encyclopedias--Juvenile literature.
Classification: DDC 796.332--dc23